Practice*Planners*

Arthur E. Jongsma, Jr., Series Editor

Helping therapists
help their clients ...

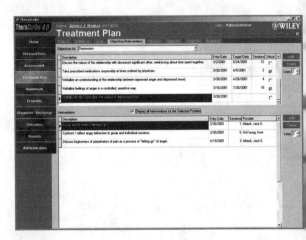

Treatment Planners cover all the necessary elements for developing formal treatment plans, including detailed problem definitions, long-term goals, short-term objectives, therapeutic interventions, and DSM-IV™ diagnoses.

❑ **The Complete Adult Psychotherapy Treatment Planner,** Third Edition
    0-471-27113-6 / $49.95

❑ **The Child Psychotherapy Treatment Planner,** Third Edition
    0-471-27050-4 / $49.95

❑ **The Adolescent Psychotherapy Treatment Planner,** Third Edition
    0-471-27049-0 / $49.95

❑ **The Couples Psychotherapy Treatment Planner**
    0-471-24711-1 / $49.95

❑ **The Employee Assistance (EAP) Treatment Planner**
    0-471-24709-X / $49.95

❑ **The Gay and Lesbian Psychotherapy Treatment Planner**
    0-471-35080-X / $49.95

❑ **The Crisis Counseling and Traumatic Events Treatment Planner**
    0-471-39587-0 / $49.95

❑ **The Social Work and Human Services Treatment Planner**
    0-471-37741-4 / $49.95

❑ **The Speech-Language Pathology Treatment Planner**
    0-471-27504-2 / $49.95

❑ **The Suicide and Homicide Risk Assessment & Prevention Treatment Planner**
    0-471-46631-X / $49.95

❑ **The Continuum of Care Treatment Planner**
    0-471-19568-5 / $49.95

❑ **The Behavioral Medicine Treatment Planner**
    0-471-31923-6 / $49.95

❑ **The Mental Retardation and Developmental Disability Treatment Planner**
    0-471-38253-1 / $49.95

❑ **The Special Education Treatment Planner**
    0-471-38872-6 / $49.95

❑ **The Severe and Persistent Mental Illness Treatment Planner**
    0-471-35945-9 / $49.95

❑ **The Personality Disorders Treatment Planner**
    0-471-39403-3 / $49.95

❑ **The Rehabilitation Psychology Treatment Planner**
    0-471-35178-4 / $49.95

❑ **The Pastoral Counseling Treatment Planner**
    0-471-25416-9 / $49.95

❑ **The Juvenile Justice and Residential Care Treatment Planner**
    0-471-43320-9 / $49.95

❑ **The Psychopharmacology Treatment Planner**
    0-471-43322-5 / $49.95

❑ **The Probation and Parole Treatment Planner**
    0-471-20244-4 / $49.95

❑ **The School Counseling and School Social Work Treatment Planner**
    0-471-08496-4 / $49.95

❑ **The Sexual Abuse Victim and Sexual Offender Treatment Planner**
    0-471-21979-7 / $49.95

❑ **The College Student Counseling Treatment Planner**
    0-471-46708-1 / $49.95

The Addiction Treatment Planner
Second Edition
    0-471-41814-5 / $49.95

The Group Therapy Treatment Planner
    0-471-37449-0 / $49.95

The Family Therapy Treatment Planner
    0-471-34768-X / $49.95

The Older Adult Psychotherapy Treatment Planner
    0-471-29574-4 / $49.95

Progress Notes Planners contain complete prewritten progress notes for each presenting problem in the companion Treatment Planners.

❑ **The Adult Psychotherapy Progress Notes Planner, 2e**
    0-471-45978-X / $49.95

❑ **The Adolescent Psychotherapy Progress Notes Planner, 2e**
    0-471-45979-8 / $49.95

❑ **The Couples Psychotherapy Progress Notes Planner**
    0-471-27460-7 / $49.95

❑ **The Child Psychotherapy Progress Notes Planner, 2e**
    0-471-45980-1 / $49.95

❑ **The Addiction Progress Notes Planner**
    0-471-10330-6 / $49.95

❑ **The Severe and Persistent Mental Illness Progress Notes Planner**
    0-471-21986-X / $49.95

Name_____

Affiliation_____

Address_____

City/State/Zip_____

Phone/Fax_____

E-mail_____

*Prices subject to change without notice.

To order, call 1-800-225-5945
(Please refer to promo #1-4019 when ordering.)

Or send this page with payment* to:
John Wiley & Sons, Inc., Attn: J. Knott
111 River Street, Hoboken, NJ 07030

❑ Check enclosed   ❑ Visa   ❑ MasterCard   ❑ American Express

Card #_____

Expiration Date_____

Signature_____

On the web: wiley.com/practiceplanners   *Please add your local sales tax to all orders.

Practice Management Tools for Busy Mental Health Professionals

Homework Planners feature dozens of behaviorally based, ready-to-use assignments that are designed for use between sessions, as well as a disk (Microsoft Word) containing all of the assignments—allowing you to customize them to suit your unique client needs.

- ☐ **Brief Therapy Homework Planner**
  0-471-24611-5 / $49.95

- ☐ **Brief Couples Therapy Homework Planner**
  0-471-29511-6 / $49.95

- ☐ **Brief Child Therapy Homework Planner**
  0-471-32366-7 / $49.95

- ☐ **Brief Adolescent Therapy Homework Planner**
  0-471-34465-6 / $49.95

- ☐ **Addiction Treatment Homework Planner, 2e**
  0-471-27459-3 / $49.95

- ☐ **Brief Employee Assistance Homework Planner**
  0-471-38088-1 / $49.95

- ☐ **Adult Psychotherapy Homework Planner**
  0-471-27395-3 / $49.95

- ☐ **Brief Family Therapy Homework Planner**
  0-471-385123-1 / $49.95

- ☐ **Grief Counseling Homework Planner**
  0-471-43318-7 / $49.95

- ☐ **Divorce Counseling Homework Planner**
  0-471-43319-5 / $49.95

- ☐ **Group Therapy Homework Planner**
  0-471-41822-6 / $49.95

- ☐ **School Counseling and School Social Work Homework Planner**
  0-471-09114-6 / $49.95

- ☐ **Child Therapy Activity and Homework Planner**
  0-471-25684-6 / $49.95

- ☐ **Adolescent Psychotherapy Homework Planner II**
  0-471-27493-3 / $49.95

Documentation Sourcebooks provide a comprehensive collection of ready-to-use blank forms, handouts, and questionnaires to help you manage your client reports and streamline the record keeping and treatment process. Features clear, concise explanations of the purpose of each form—including when it should be used and at what point. Includes customizable forms on disk.

- ☐ **The Clinical Documentation Sourcebook,**
  Second Edition
  0-471-32692-5 / $49.95

- ☐ **The Psychotherapy Documentation Primer**
  0-471-28990-6 / $45.00

- ☐ **The Couple and Family Clinical Documentation Sourcebook**
  0-471-25234-4 / $49.95

- ☐ **The Clinical Child Documentation Sourcebook**
  0-471-29111-0 / $49.95

- ☐ **The Chemical Dependence Treatment Documentation Sourcebook**
  0-471-31285-1 / $49.95

- ☐ **The Forensic Documentation Sourcebook**
  0-471-25459-2 / $95.00

- ☐ **The Continuum of Care Clinical Documentation Sourcebook**
  0-471-34581-4 / $85.00

To order by phone, call TOLL FREE 1-800-225-5945

Or contact us at:
John Wiley & Sons, Inc., Attn: J. Knott
111 River Street, Hoboken, NJ 07030
Fax: 1-800-597-3299
Online: www.wiley.com/practiceplanners

The College Student Counseling Treatment Planner

PracticePlanners® Series

Treatment Planners

The Complete Adult Psychotherapy Treatment Planner, Third Edition
The Child Psychotherapy Treatment Planner, Third Edition
The Adolescent Psychotherapy Treatment Planner, Third Edition
The Addiction Treatment Planner, Second Edition
The Continuum of Care Treatment Planner
The Couples Psychotherapy Treatment Planner
The Employee Assistance Treatment Planner
The Pastoral Counseling Treatment Planner
The Older Adult Psychotherapy Treatment Planner
The Behavioral Medicine Treatment Planner
The Group Therapy Treatment Planner
The Gay and Lesbian Psychotherapy Treatment Planner
The Family Therapy Treatment Planner
The Severe and Persistent Mental Illness Treatment Planner
The Mental Retardation and Developmental Disability Treatment Planner
The Social Work and Human Services Treatment Planner
The Crisis Counseling and Traumatic Events Treatment Planner
The Personality Disorders Treatment Planner
The Rehabilitation Psychology Treatment Planner
The Special Education Treatment Planner
The Juvenile Justice and Residential Care Treatment Planner
The School Counseling and School Social Work Treatment Planner
The Sexual Abuse Victim and Sexual Offender Treatment Planner
The Probation and Parole Treatment Planner
The Psychopharmacology Treatment Planner
The Speech-Language Pathology Treatment Planner
The Suicide and Homicide Risk Assessment & Prevention Treatment Planner
The College Student Counseling Treatment Planner

Progress Note Planners

The Child Psychotherapy Progress Notes Planner, Second Edition
The Adolescent Psychotherapy Progress Notes Planner, Second Edition
The Adult Psychotherapy Progress Notes Planner, Second Edition
The Addiction Progress Notes Planner
The Severe and Persistent Mental Illness Progress Notes Planner
The Couples Psychotherapy Progress Notes Planner
The Family Therapy Progress Notes Planner

Homework Planners

Brief Therapy Homework Planner
Brief Couples Therapy Homework Planner
Brief Adolescent Therapy Homework Planner
Brief Child Therapy Homework Planner
Brief Employee Assistance Homework Planner
Brief Family Therapy Homework Planner
Grief Counseling Homework Planner
Group Therapy Homework Planner
Divorce Counseling Homework Planner
School Counseling and School Social Work Homework Planner
Child Therapy Activity and Homework Planner
Addiction Treatment Homework Planner, Second Edition
Adolescent Psychotherapy Homework Planner II
Adult Psychotherapy Homework Planner

Client Education Handout Planners

Adult Client Education Handout Planner
Child and Adolescent Client Education Handout Planner
Couples and Family Client Education Handout Planner

Documentation Sourcebooks

The Clinical Documentation Sourcebook, Second Edition
The Forensic Documentation Sourcebook
The Psychotherapy Documentation Primer
The Chemical Dependence Treatment Documentation Sourcebook
The Couple and Family Clinical Documentation Sourcebook
The Continuum of Care Clinical Documentation Sourcebook

Complete Planners

The Complete Depression Treatment and Homework Planner
The Complete Anxiety Treatment and Homework Planner

PracticePlanners®

Arthur E. Jongsma, Jr., Series Editor

The College Student Counseling Treatment Planner

Camille Helkowski

Chris E. Stout

Arthur E. Jongsma, Jr.

WILEY

JOHN WILEY & SONS, INC.

Published by John Wiley & Sons, Inc., Hoboken, New Jersey.
Published simultaneously in Canada.

For general information on our other products and services please contact our Customer Care Department within the United States at (800) 762-2974, outside the United States at (317) 572-3993 or fax (317) 572-4002.

Wiley also publishes its books in a variety of electronic formats. Some content that appears in print may not be available in electronic books. For more information about Wiley products, visit our Web site at www.wiley.com.

Library of Congress Cataloging-in-Publication Data:

Helkowski, Camille.
   The college student counseling treatment planner / Camille Helkowski, Chris Stout,
   Arthur E. Jongsma.
      p.   cm. — (Practice planners series)
   Includes bibliographical references.
   ISBN 0-471-46708-1 (pbk.)
      1. College students—Mental health services.   2. Counseling in higher education.
   3. College students—Counseling of—Planning.   4. Psychotherapy. I. Stout, Chris E.
   II. Jongsma, Arthur E., 1943– III. Title. IV. Practice planners
   RC451.4.S7 H455   2004
   378.1′9713—dc22

                                                                                    2003021214

Printed in the United States of America.

10   9   8   7   6   5   4   3   2   1

To my students, who have always been my best teachers.
—C.H.

To my ever-understanding mother-in-law, Mary Louise
(Wentz) Beckstrand, whose Door County, Wisconsin,
home became a wonderful retreat for my writing projects.
—C.E.S.

In memory of my mother, Harmina Doot, whose
sacrificial love and joyful spirit continues to glow in the
hearts of her family.
—A.E.J.

CONTENTS

PRACTICE*PLANNERS*® SERIES PREFACE

The practice of psychotherapy has a dimension that did not exist 30, 20, or even 15 years ago—accountability. Treatment programs, public agencies, clinics, and even group and solo practitioners must now justify the treatment of patients to outside review entities that control the payment of fees. This development has resulted in an explosion of paperwork. Clinicians must now document what has been done in treatment, what is planned for the future, and what the anticipated outcomes of the interventions are. The books and software in this Practice*Planners* series are designed to help practitioners fulfill these documentation requirements efficiently and professionally.

The Practice*Planners* series is growing rapidly. It now includes not only the original *The Complete Adult Psychotherapy Treatment Planner,* Third Edition, *The Child Psychotherapy Treatment Planner,* Third Edition, and *The Adolescent Psychotherapy Treatment Planner*, Third Edition, but also Treatment Planners targeted to specialty areas of practice, including: addictions, juvenile justice/residential care, couples therapy, employee assistance, behavioral medicine, therapy with older adults, pastoral counseling, family therapy, group therapy, neuropsychology, therapy with gays and lesbians, special education, school counseling, probation and parole, therapy with sexual abuse victims and offenders, and more.

Several of the Treatment Planner books now have companion Progress Notes Planners (e.g., Adult, Adolescent, Child, Addictions, Severe and Persistent Mental Illness, Couples). More of these planners that provide a menu of progress statements that elaborate on the client's symptom presentation and the provider's therapeutic intervention are in production. Each Progress Notes Planner statement is directly integrated with "Behavioral Definitions" and "Therapeutic Interventions" items from the companion Treatment Planner.

The list of therapeutic Homework Planners is also growing from the original Brief Therapy Homework for Adult to Adolescent, Child, Couples, Group, Family, Addictions, Divorce, Grief, Employee Assistance, and School Counseling/School Social Work Homework Planners. Each of these books can be used alone or in conjunction with their companion Treatment Planner. Homework assignments are designed around each presenting problem (e.g., Anxiety, Depression, Chemical Dependence, Anger

Management, Panic, Eating Disorders) that is the focus of a chapter in its corresponding Treatment Planner.

Client Education Handout Planners, a new branch in the series, provides brochures and handouts to help educate and inform adult, child, adolescent, couples, and family clients on a myriad of mental health issues, as well as life skills techniques. The list of presenting problems for which information is provided mirrors the list of presenting problems in the Treatment Planner of the title similar to that of the Handout Planner. Thus, the problems for which educational material is provided in the *Child and Adolescent Client Education Handout Planner* reflect the presenting problems listed in *The Child* and *The Adolescent Psychotherapy Treatment Planner* books. Handouts are included on CD-ROMs for easy printing and are ideal for use in waiting rooms, at presentations, as newsletters, or as information for clients struggling with mental illness issues.

In addition, the series also includes Thera*Scribe*®, the latest version of the popular treatment planning, clinical record-keeping software. Thera*Scribe* allows the user to import the data from any of the Treatment Planner, Progress Notes Planner, or Homework Planner books into the software's expandable database. Then the point-and-click method can create a detailed, neatly organized, individualized, and customized treatment plan along with optional integrated progress notes and homework assignments.

Adjunctive books, such as *The Psychotherapy Documentation Primer*, and *Clinical, Forensic, Child, Couples and Family, Continuum of Care*, and *Chemical Dependence Documentation Sourcebook* contain forms and resources to aid the mental health practice management. The goal of the series is to provide practitioners with the resources they need to provide high-quality care in the era of accountability—or, to put it simply, we seek to help you spend more time on patients, and less time on paperwork.

ARTHUR E. JONGSMA, JR.
Grand Rapids, Michigan

ACKNOWLEDGMENTS

We would like to thank Peggy Alexander for her ever-professional job of combining wonderful teams of authors. We are fortunate to be a part of such a team. Art Jongsma and Jen Byrne, his manuscript manager, have been the best.

—C.H. and C.E.S.

Each book in the Practice*Planner* series is a joint effort between uniquely qualified experts in a specific field and myself. This treatment planner book is no exception. Cam Helkowski and Chris Stout have brought their mental health expertise to focus on a topic that has received increased public attention recently, college student counseling. These two coauthors were wonderful to work with and always prompt, open to suggestions, and thoroughly professional. Thank you Cam and Chris.

My publishing team at Wiley, Peggy Alexander, David Bernstein, Judi Knott, Cris Wojdylo, and Micheline Frederick, continue to provide enthusiastic support to this Practice*Planner* project as it enters its tenth year. Thank you all.

—A.E.J.

INTRODUCTION

Since the early 1960s, formalized treatment planning has gradually become a vital aspect of the health-care delivery system, whether it is treatment related to physical health, mental health, child welfare, or substance abuse. What started in the medical sector in the 1960s spread into the mental health sector in the 1970s as clinics, psychiatric hospitals, agencies, and so on, began to seek accreditation from bodies such as the Joint Commission on Accreditation of Healthcare Organizations (JCAHO) to qualify for third-party reimbursements.

With the advent of managed care in the 1980s, treatment planning took on even more importance. Managed care systems *insist* that clinicians move rapidly from assessment of the problem to the formulation and implementation of the treatment plan. The goal of most managed care companies is to expedite the treatment process by prompting the client and treatment provider to focus on identifying and changing behavioral problems as quickly as possible. Treatment plans must be specific as to the presenting problems, behaviorally defined symptoms, treatment goals and objectives, and interventions. Treatment plans must be individualized to meet the client's needs and goals, and the observable objectives must allow for setting milestones that can be used to chart the client's progress. Pressure from third-party payors, accrediting agencies, and other outside parties has therefore increased the need for clinicians to produce effective, high-quality treatment plans in a short time frame. However, many mental health providers have little experience in treatment plan development. Our purpose in writing this book is to clarify, simplify, and accelerate the treatment planning process.

PLANNER FOCUS

The College Student Counseling Treatment Planner is designed for counselors, social workers, psychologists, and other mental health specialists who provide guidance, counseling, and therapeutic support to college students. It incorporates presenting problems as an extensive representation of the social-emotional, behavioral, academic, and interpersonal challenges that college students struggle with as they move through their college careers.

The college student population is comprised of young adults (aged 18 to 30) from a range of life circumstances. Their presenting issues are diverse and tend to be a mix of developmental, transitional, and mental health concerns. Given these factors, interventions were designed to offer a variety of meaningful strategies to improve the quality of the student's educational and social/emotional experience. The interventions target the student's functioning on campus, in social settings, and in the community. Reality-based therapeutic interventions are offered in support of the following goals: to encourage the student's ability to develop intellectual, physical, and personal competence; effectively manage positive and negative emotions; understand and embrace emotional interdependence and the capacity to be both separate and connected to others; establish an identity with core characteristics (body, sexuality, self-concept in a social and cultural context) that are consistent and congruent; and embrace a sense of purpose and a lifestyle that reflects the student's beliefs about the self and the world (Chickering and Reisser, 1993).

HISTORICAL BACKGROUND

A 2000/2001 survey conducted by the International Association of Counseling Services reported that 90% of the 274 participating college and university counseling centers hospitalized at least one student for mental health problems; and, 30% of the schools reported at least one student suicide. A 2001 Massachusetts Institute of Technology task force found that 74% of the students surveyed said that they had an emotional problem that interfered with their daily lives. This second finding, while certainly less dramatic than hospitalization or suicide, confirms the intensity of the demand for a broad range of counseling services. It is clear that students, their families, and the entire university community expect clinicians to respond skillfully and swiftly to whatever comes their way.

Mental health professionals working with college students are faced with some gray areas particular to the population they serve. The largest developmental task of young adulthood is bringing identity into focus. While answering the question, "Who am I?" is a life-long undertaking, it is the front-and-center issue for the young adult. Campus life provides a myriad of opportunities to test the identity waters. A body of literature suggests that young adulthood can be viewed as a unique developmental stage complete with specific developmental tasks (Chickering and Reisser, 1969, 1993; Erikson, 1963, 1968, 1980; Marcia, 1966, 1980; Parks, 2000).

The majority of college student's fall into this category. This requires that clinicians be skillful and comfortable operating in the gray zone of developmental testing and experimentation. The point at which developmental struggles turn into mental health concerns is not always clearly marked. This decision must be made in the context of a client's history and the campus culture. Keeping developmental factors, personal history, and campus mores in mind can cast a client's behaviors in a different light and prevent clinicians from identifying pathology where none exists.

Dovetailing with developmental tasks of young adulthood are the transitions of college life. A number of key transitions occur in a very short span of time; and, often, they come too quickly to be anticipated or clearly understood by the young adults that must live through them. Most students arrive at orientation as children living in their family home; and, within a few days, they experience a type of independence only enjoyed by college students. The freedoms a typical college student possesses include: large blocks of completely unstructured time; little or no supervision of their sleeping, eating, socializing, or study habits; first-time access to credit while financial obligations are subsidized in part or fully by others.

Initially, there are few behavioral limits and even fewer benchmarks of developmental progress. Grades may only be given at the end of the term with little to no feedback in the course of the semester. There may be the occasional disciplinary write-up from a residence hall staff member or questions from a concerned roommate or classmate that can—but not always—serve as warnings. While freshmen are coping with these freedoms, they are also facing some losses. They may miss their families and friends at home. Their life-long support structures are suddenly gone, and the ones they will build at college have not yet been constructed. Considering the enormity of this initial transition, it is amazing that most college students get through it as well as they do.

While these first transitions are obvious, others are not. Choosing a major and thinking about career options are often difficult and stressful for college students, no matter what their chronological age. Students also are faced with tough choices about relationships, emotional and physical intimacy, sexual orientation, use of alcohol and other drugs, appropriate management of emotions, and a host of other issues. While they have made these choices before, they typically weren't flying solo when they made them. Someone else was there to hold them accountable in the moment. At school, they are completely in charge of their lives and are completely responsible—not only for their choices but also for the corresponding short- and long-term consequences. Again, transition issues coincide with developmental tasks.

On receipt of a diploma, full-time student status gives way to full-time employment. Financial independence is no longer optional, a ready-made community is not always available, and there are no grades to mark their career or personal progress. While few students have been told that making it in the real world is easy, even fewer feel completely ready for this transition. College students need access to both the information and support to negotiate the rapids of transitional and developmental change.

The College Student Counseling Treatment Planner seeks to provide a menu of statements that define the student's problem, set goals for treatment, outline objectives for the student to achieve in counseling, and briefly describe interventions that the counselor may use to assist the student in making progress toward the objectives (as always, intervention numbers are placed in parentheses after each objective as a way to suggest which intervention may be most appropriate for the specific objective). Finally, *DSM-IV-TR* Diagnostic Suggestions associated with the presenting problem are placed at the end of each chapter. Clinicians should respond quickly to students presenting problems of depression, anxiety, addiction, or other mental health issues. Sometimes, the move to college provides the distance and safety required for students to allow their previously untreated issues to surface. This is often the case for students with a history of abuse and/or neglect.

QUANTIFIED TREATMENT PLANNING

With increased expectations on clinical performance, regardless of setting or therapeutic orientation, there is an increased emphasis on behaviorally observable and/or quantifiable aspects of treatment plans. Counselors may want to look for the opportunity to craft measurable/quantifiable aspects of the client's behaviors into their treatment plans. This can be accomplished by introducing measurability at the symptomatic level (e.g., Behavioral Definitions) and/or at the treatment outcome level (e.g., Short-Term Objectives). Behavioral Definition terms such as *repeated, frequent, tendency, pattern, consistent, excessive, high-level, persistent, displays, heightened, recurrent,* and the like, and even words like *verbalizes, displays, demonstrates, refuses, unable, avoids, seeks, difficulty, increasing,* or *declining* can all have frequencies or circumstances added to quantify the item. For example, the Definition item "Verbalizes having suicidal ideation" can be made more quantifiably measurable by changing it to "Verbalizes having suicidal ideation once to twice daily for the past two weeks."

Counselors also may add aspects of severity to symptom Definition statements to introduce greater measurability. For example, "Verbalizes having sad thoughts 4 to 5 times daily for the past two weeks, and, on a scale from 1 to 10 (10 being worst), were judged to be at an 8 or higher." Or, alternatively, the clinician may list quantified psychometric data as a criterion measure, such as scores from symptom screening instruments such as the Brief Psychiatric Rating System (BPRS), Beck Depression Inventory (BDI), Hamilton-Depression Inventory (Ham-D), Brief Symptom Index (BSI), Symptom Checklist-90-Revised (SCL-90-R), or Global Assessment of Functioning (GAF). This helps in decreasing subjectivity as well.

The Short-Term Objective language found in the *Treatment Planner* can also be modified to follow the more quantified approach; thus, "Engage in physical and recreational activities that reflect increased energy and interest" becomes "Engage in physical and recreational activities that reflect increased energy and interest, at least 5 times per shift within one week's time (by 1/20/2005)." Also, "Verbally express understanding of the relationship between depressed mood and repression of sadness and anger" becomes "Verbally express understanding of the relationship between depressed mood and repression of sadness and anger (by 1/18/2005)."

At the end of this Introduction, we have included two sample treatment plans to illustrate how a plan's language can be modified to make it more quantifiable. The first plan uses standard language, and the second plan has been revised into more specific, observable, quantifiable terms. This revised example serves as a guide for the practitioner who wishes to qualify his or her treatment plans.

Finally, in Appendix A we have included an entire chapter revised into more specific, measurable, quantifiable language. The Academic Underachievement chapter in Appendix A adds greater measurability to Behavioral Definition statements and to Short-Term Objective statements. This chapter provides a guide for those who would like to modify the language used throughout the other chapters.

DEVELOPING A TREATMENT PLAN

The process of developing a treatment plan involves a logical series of steps that build on each other much like constructing a house. The foundation of any effective treatment plan is the data gathered in a thorough biopsychosocial assessment. As the client presents himself or herself for treatment, the clinician must sensitively listen to and understand what the client struggles with in terms of family-of-origin issues, current stressors, emotional status, social network, physical health, coping skills, interpersonal conflicts, self-esteem, and so on. Assessment data may be gathered from a social history, physical exam, clinical interview, psychological testing, or contact with a client's significant others. The integration of the data by the clinician or the multidisciplinary treatment team members is critical for understanding the client, as is an awareness of the basis of the client's struggle. We have identified six specific steps for developing an effective treatment plan based on the assessment data.

Step One: Problem Selection

Although the client may discuss a variety of issues during the assessment, the clinician must determine the most significant problems on which to focus the treatment process. Usually a *primary* problem will surface, although *secondary* problems may also be evident. *Other* problems may have to be set aside as not urgent enough to require treatment at this time. An effective treatment plan can only deal with a few selected problems or treatment will lose its direction. This *Planner* offers 28 problems from which to select those that most accurately represent your client's presenting issues.

As the problems to be selected become clear to the clinician or the treatment team, it is important to include opinions from the client as to his or her prioritization of issues for which help is being sought. A client's motivation to participate in and cooperate with the treatment process depends, to some extent, on the degree to which treatment addresses his or her greatest needs.

Step Two: Problem Definition

Each individual client presents with unique nuances as to how a problem behaviorally reveals itself in his or her life. Therefore, each problem that is selected for treatment focus requires a specific definition about how it is evidenced in the particular client. The symptom pattern should be associated with diagnostic criteria and codes such as those found in the *Diagnostic and Statistical Manual, Text Revision (DSM-IV-TR)* or the *International Classification of Diseases*. This *Planner,* following the pattern established by *DSM-IV-TR,* offers behaviorally specific definition statements to choose from or to serve as a model for your own personally crafted statements. You will find several behavior symptoms or syndromes listed that may characterize one of the 28 presenting problems.

Step Three: Goal Development

The next step in treatment plan development is to set broad goals for the resolution of the target problem. These statements need not be crafted in measurable terms but can be global, long-term goals that indicate a desired positive outcome to the treatment procedures. The *Planner* suggests several possible goal statements for each problem, but one statement is all that is required in a treatment plan.

Step Four: Objective Construction

In contrast to long-term goals, objectives must be stated in behaviorally measurable language. It must be clear when the client has achieved the established objectives; therefore, vague, subjective objectives are not acceptable. Review agencies (e.g., JCAHO), HMOs, and managed care organizations insist that psychological treatment outcomes be measurable. The objectives presented in this *Planner* are designed to meet this demand for accountability. Numerous alternatives are presented to allow construction of a variety of treatment plan possibilities for the same presenting problem. The clinician must exercise professional judgment as to which objectives are most appropriate for a given client.

Each objective should be developed as a step toward attaining the broad treatment goal. In essence, objectives can be thought of as a series of steps that, when completed, will result in the achievement of the long-term goal. There should be at least two objectives for each problem, but the clinician may construct as many as are necessary for goal achievement. Target attainment dates may be listed for each objective. New objectives should be added to the plan as the individual's treatment progresses. When all the necessary objectives have been achieved, the client should have resolved the target problem successfully.

Step Five: Intervention Creation

Interventions are the actions of the clinician designed to help the client complete the objectives. There should be at least one intervention for every objective. If the client does not accomplish the objective after the initial intervention, new interventions should be added to the plan.

Interventions should be selected on the basis of the client's needs and the treatment provider's full therapeutic repertoire. This *Planner* contains interventions from a broad range of therapeutic approaches, including cognitive, dynamic, behavioral, pharmacologic, family-oriented, and solution-focused brief therapy. Other interventions may be written by the provider to reflect his or her own training and experience. The addition of new problems, definitions, goals, objectives, and interventions to those found in the *Planner* is encouraged because doing so adds to the database for future reference and use.

Some suggested interventions listed in the *Planner* refer to specific books that can be assigned to the client for adjunctive bibliotherapy. Appendix B contains a full bibliographic reference list of these materials.

The books are arranged under each problem for which they are appropriate as assigned reading for clients. When a book is used as part of an intervention plan, it should be reviewed with the client after it is read, enhancing the application of the content of the book to the specific client's circumstances. For further information about self-help books, mental health professionals may wish to consult *The Authoritative Guide to Self-Help Books* (2003) by Santrock, Minnett, and Campbell (available from The Guilford Press, New York).

Assigning an intervention to a specific provider is most relevant if the client is being treated by a team in an inpatient, residential, or intensive outpatient setting. Within these settings, personnel other than the primary clinician may be responsible for implementing a specific intervention. Review agencies require that the responsible provider's name be stipulated for every intervention.

Step Six: Diagnosis Determination

The determination of an appropriate diagnosis is based on an evaluation of the client's complete clinical presentation. The clinician must compare the behavioral, cognitive, emotional, and interpersonal symptoms that the client presents to the criteria for diagnosis of a mental illness condition as described in *DSM-IV-TR*. The issue of differential diagnosis is admittedly a difficult one that research has shown to have rather low interrater reliability. Many mental health professionals are also trained to think more in terms of maladaptive behavior than in disease labels. In spite of these factors, diagnosis is a reality that exists in the world of mental health care, and it is a necessity for third-party reimbursement. (However, recently, managed care agencies are more interested in behavioral indices that are exhibited by the client than in the actual diagnosis.) It is the clinician's thorough knowledge of *DSM-IV-TR* criteria and a complete understanding of the client assessment data that contribute to the most reliable, valid diagnosis. An accurate assessment of behavioral indicators will also contribute to more effective treatment planning.

HOW TO USE THIS PLANNER

Our experience has taught us that learning the skills of effective treatment plan writing can be a tedious and difficult process for many clinicians. It is more stressful to try to develop this expertise when under the pressure of increased client load and short time frames placed on clinicians today by managed care systems. The documentation demands can be overwhelming when we must move quickly from assessment to treatment plan to progress notes. In the process, we must be very specific about how and when objectives can be achieved, and how progress is exhibited in each client. *The College Student Counseling Treatment Planner* was developed as a tool to aid clinicians in writing a treatment plan in a rapid manner that is clear, specific, and highly individualized according to the following progression:

1. Choose one presenting problem (Step One) you have identified through your assessment process. Locate the corresponding page number for that problem in the *Planner*'s table of contents.
2. Select two or three of the listed behavioral definitions (Step Two) and record them in the appropriate section on your treatment plan form. Feel free to add your own defining statement if you determine that your client's behavioral manifestation of the identified problem is not listed. (Note that while our design for treatment planning is vertical, it will work equally well on plan forms formatted horizontally.)
3. Select a single long-term goal (Step Three) and again write the selection, exactly as it is written in the *Planner* or in some appropriately modified form, in the corresponding area of your own form.
4. Review the listed objectives for this problem and select the ones that you judge to be clinically indicated for your client (Step Four). Remember, it is recommended that you select at least two objectives for each problem. Add a target date or the number of sessions allocated for the attainment of each objective.
5. Choose relevant interventions (Step Five). The *Planner* offers suggested interventions related to each objective in the parentheses following the objective statement. But do not limit yourself to those interventions. The entire list is eclectic and may offer options that are more tailored to your theoretical approach or preferred way of working with clients. Also, just as with definitions, goals, and objectives, there is space allowed for you to enter your own interventions into the *Planner.* This allows you to refer to these entries when you create a plan around this problem in the future. You will have to assign responsibility to a specific person for implementation of each intervention if the treatment is being carried out by a multidisciplinary team.
6. Several *DSM-IV-TR* diagnoses are listed at the end of each chapter that are commonly associated with a client who has this problem. These diagnoses are meant to be suggestions for clinical consideration. Select a diagnosis listed or assign a more appropriate choice from the *DSM-IV-TR* (Step Six).

To accommodate those practitioners who tend to plan treatment in terms of diagnostic labels rather than presenting problems, Appendix C lists all of the *DSM-IV-TR* diagnoses that have been presented in the various presenting problem chapters for consideration. Each diagnosis is followed by the presenting problem that has been associated with that diagnosis. The provider may look up the presenting problems for a selected diagnosis to review definitions, goals, objectives, and interventions that may be appropriate for their clients with that diagnosis.

Congratulations! You should now have a complete, individualized treatment plan that is ready for immediate implementation and presentation to the client. It should resemble the format of the "Sample Standard Treatment Plan" presented on page 11. This same treatment plan has been revised to include more quantifiable terms and this "Sample Quantified Treatment Plan" is presented on page 14.

A FINAL NOTE

For college students, all mental health concerns must be viewed in the context of personal history, campus culture, transitions being experienced, and developmental tasks at hand. Diagnostic labeling may not always be the most useful or most appropriate approach. At best, good diagnosis is a risky business and at worst it is harmful to the client. It may be better to diagnose with great discretion, while intervening quickly on more obvious symptoms. We hope that *The College Student Counseling Treatment Planner* helps you intervene effectively and efficiently.

SAMPLE STANDARD TREATMENT PLAN

PROBLEM: ACADEMIC UNDERACHIEVEMENT

Definitions: Has thoughts about assignments and/or tests that provoke feelings of anxiety and prevent optimum academic performance.

Expresses fear of failure that leads to avoidance of allocating the necessary time and effort to studying.

Goals: Learn and implement stress-management skills to reduce academic performance anxiety.

Employ time-management and goal-setting skills necessary for academic success.

OBJECTIVES

1. Clarify the facts, beliefs, and feelings about academic ability and performance and discuss in session.

2. Explore the impact of personal belief system on academic behaviors.

INTERVENTIONS

1. Explore the student's beliefs about his/her academic ability and performance; review his/her history of academic performance (e.g., GPA, grade transcript, or number of classes enrolled in per term).

2. Help the student identify and clarify feelings (e.g., anxiety, doubt, frustration, guilt, joy, pride, or shame) generated by his/her beliefs about academic ability and performance.

1. Help the student evaluate each of his/her beliefs about his/her academic performance using the questions, "Is this a reasonable (rational) expectation?" and "Is this an achievable expectation?" as criteria.

	2. Assist the student in recognizing the connection between irrational and/or unachievable academic beliefs or expectations and the emotional struggles and academic problems he/she is currently experiencing.
3. Restructure academic expectations, making them rational and conducive to constructive academic behaviors.	1. Assign the student homework of revising his/her belief statements, making each statement more reasonable and achievable (e.g., "I am committed to maintaining a 2.8 to 3.5 GPA each semester" or "I can improve my math performance and will do so by utilizing the learning assistance resources provided on campus").
	2. Ask the student to identify and record positive emotional reactions and academic behaviors that each revised belief statement would generate.
4. Identify the debilitating effects of high anxiety levels on academic performance.	1. Teach the student about the debilitating effects of anxiety on academic performance (e.g., increased distractibility, reduced ability to recall material, increased strength of negative outcome expectations, preoccupation with physiological aspects of anxiety [increased heart rate, perspiration, shallow breathing, or dizziness], or fatigue from muscle tension and sleep disturbance).
5. Identify and address the suspected causes of performance anxiety.	1. Assist the student in identifying the causes of his/her debilitating performance anxiety (e.g., unreasonable personal beliefs or expectations about academic performance, unreasonable expectations from parents, past failure experiences, recent adjustment problems to life on campus,

lack of tutorial assistance for new and difficult material, or poor study skills or time management).

2. Develop a plan to address the identified causes of the student's performance anxiety (e.g., replace irrational beliefs about academic performance, confront parental expectations directly, apply problem solving to campus life issues of conflict, access campus-based tutoring services, implement effective study skills or time-management procedures).

6. Implement relaxation techniques to reduce test-taking stress.

1. Teach the student relaxation skills (e.g., deep muscle release, deep breathing, or progressive relaxation) to implement at times of high test anxiety or general performance stress.

2. Teach the student the use of positive imagery techniques (e.g., imagining a relaxing scene of laying on a beach under the warm sun, full and clear recall of facts during a test situation, or successful enactment of skills in front of a group) to induce calm, relaxation, and a sense of peace during times of high test or performance anxiety.

3. Use role-playing to help the student apply relaxation and positive imagery skills to specific debilitating performance anxiety situations.

Diagnosis: 309.24   Adjustment Disorder with Anxiety

SAMPLE QUANTITATIVE TREATMENT PLAN

PROBLEM: ACADEMIC UNDERACHIEVEMENT

BEHAVIORAL DEFINITIONS

1. Has thoughts about assignments and/or tests occurring ___ times per day that provoke feelings of anxiety and prevent optimal academic performance.
2. Expresses fear of failure that leads to avoidance of allocating the necessary time and effort to studying that occurs ___ times per day (or that occurs ___ times per course).

LONG-TERM GOALS

1. Learn and implement stress-management skills to reduce academic performance anxiety.
2. Employ the time-management and goal-setting skills necessary for academic success.

SHORT-TERM OBJECTIVES	THERAPEUTIC INTERVENTIONS
1. By _____ (enter date), the student will clarify the facts, beliefs, and feelings about academic ability and performance and discuss in session.	1. Explore the student's beliefs about his/her academic ability and performance; review his/her history of academic performance (e.g., GPA, grade transcript, or number of classes enrolled in per term).

2. Help the student identify and clarify feelings (e.g., anxiety, doubt, frustration, guilt, joy, pride, or shame) generated by his/her beliefs about academic ability and performance.

2. By _____ (enter date), the student will explore the impact of his/her personal belief system on academic behaviors.

1. Help the student evaluate each of his/her beliefs about his/her academic performance using the questions, "Is this a reasonable (rational) expectation?" and "Is this an achievable expectation?" as criteria.

2. Assist the student in recognizing the connection between irrational and/or unachievable academic beliefs or expectations and the emotional struggles and academic problems he/she is currently experiencing.

3. By _____ (enter date), the student will restructure academic expectations, making them rational and conducive to constructive academic behaviors.

1. Assign the student homework of revising his/her belief statements, making each statement more reasonable and achievable (e.g., "I am committed to maintaining a 2.8 to 3.5 GPA each semester" or "I can improve my math performance and will do so by utilizing the learning assistance resources provided on campus").

2. Ask the student to identify and record positive emotional reactions and academic behaviors that each revised belief statement would generate.

4. By _____ (enter date), the student will identify the debilitating effects of high anxiety levels on academic performance with specific examples as to which courses and/or professors.

1. Teach the student about the debilitating effects of anxiety on academic performance (e.g., increased distractibility, reduced ability to recall material, increased strength of negative outcome expectations,

preoccupation with physiological aspects of anxiety [increased heart rate, perspiration, shallow breathing, or dizziness], or fatigue from muscle tension and sleep disturbance).

5. By _____ (enter date), the student will identify and address the suspected causes of performance anxiety.

1. Assist the student in identifying the causes of his/her debilitating performance anxiety (e.g., unreasonable personal beliefs or expectations about academic performance, unreasonable expectations from parents, past failure experiences, recent adjustment problems to life on campus, lack of tutorial assistance for new and difficult material, or poor study skills or time management).

2. Develop a plan to address the identified causes of the student's performance anxiety (e.g., replace irrational beliefs about academic performance, confront parental expectations directly, apply problem solving to campus life issues of conflict, access campus-based tutoring services, implement effective study skills or time-management procedures).

6. By _____ (enter date), the student will implement relaxation techniques to reduce test-taking stress by ___%.

1. Teach the student relaxation skills (e.g., deep muscle release, deep breathing, or progressive relaxation) to implement at times of high test anxiety or general performance stress.

2. Teach the student the use of positive imagery techniques (e.g., imagining a relaxing scene of laying on a beach under the warm sun, full and clear recall of facts during a test situation, or

successful enactment of skills in front of a group) to induce calm, relaxation, and a sense of peace during times of high test or performance anxiety.

3. Use role-playing to help the student apply relaxation and positive imagery skills to specific debilitating performance anxiety situations.

DIAGNOSTIC SUGGESTIONS:

Axis I: 309.24   Adjustment Disorder with Anxiety

ABUSIVE RELATIONSHIPS

BEHAVIORAL DEFINITIONS

1. Avoids displeasing or angering the partner at all costs (e.g., misses classes or work, stops socializing with friends, or yields control of personal time and money to partner).
2. Feels intimidated by interactions with partner leading to pervasive worry, anxiety, and/or fear.
3. Attempts to control others and the environment to prevent anything that could serve as a catalyst for the partner's anger/violence.
4. Experiences feelings of inadequacy, guilt, and shame in reaction to the partner's constant criticism, belittling comments, and/or demeaning demands.
5. Feels invisible and/or unworthy because ideas, interests, and needs are ignored or dismissed by the partner.
6. Excuses the partner's abusive physical and sexual behavior and blames self for creating a situation in which the partner could not control rage and violent impulses.
7. Sustains physical injuries at the hands of the partner and lies to medical personnel and friends about the origin of the injuries.
8. Isolates self from family, friends, and campus personnel due to feelings of embarrassment and fear.
9. Believes that it is impossible to leave the relationship due to financial, emotional, and/or social dependence on the partner.
10. Believes that it is impossible to leave the relationship due to the partner's threats of physical violence, death, and/or suicide.

—. _____

_____

—. _____

_____

—. _____

_____

LONG-TERM GOALS

1. Terminate the abusive relationship and accept that no one deserves to be victimized by abuse.
2. Reclaim a personal vision of self as deserving kindness and respect.
3. Articulate his or her own views and perspectives independent of the partner's dictums.
4. Understand the impact of an abusive relationship on identity development and engage in behaviors that are emotionally and physically nurturing and strengthening.
5. Renew relationships with family, friends, and other sources of support, affirmation, and comfort.
6. Create and maintain healthy boundaries in intimate relationships.
7. Recommit to academic goals and create a plan of action.

—. _____

_____

—. _____

_____

—. _____

_____

SHORT-TERM OBJECTIVES	THERAPEUTIC INTERVENTIONS
1. Describe the immediate abusive situation that precipitated seeking assistance. (1, 2, 3)	1. Explore the particular abusive incident or current situation that led the student to seek counseling.
	2. Assess the level of danger to the student (e.g., is the partner violent; has the abuse been increasing lately; has the partner threatened to harm or kill the student, someone in the student's family, or him/herself; or does the partner have a weapon); contact campus safety and security, the police, and/or other crisis intervention personnel to ensure his/her immediate safety.

	3. Encourage the student to utilize the student health center, campus legal clinic, or other campus/community services to ensure his/her safety and well-being.
2. Describe the history and results of the abusive relationship. (4, 5, 6)	4. Explore the history of and feelings about the student's relationship with his/her abusive partner.
	5. Encourage the student to describe the initial incidents that were indicative of the partner's potential for abuse.
	6. Explore the student's abusive incidents in depth and assist him/her in identifying relationship patterns that led to or resulted from the abuse and the effects of the abuse on his/her self-esteem.
3. Sort out and identify the feelings that are generated by this abusive relationship. (7, 8, 9)	7. Clarify the types of feelings that are typically generated by an abusive relationship (e.g., anxiety, self-blame, fear, embarrassment, or shame) for the student.
	8. Assist the student in identifying, as specifically as possible, his/her own feelings about the abuse and help him/her normalize them.
	9. Encourage the student to use a journal to record his/her feelings and thoughts about this relationship; ask him/her to recall in the journal any previous relationships that have generated similar emotions and thinking.
4. Verbalize an understanding of the facts about abusive relationships, in general. (10)	10. Provide the student with facts about abusive relationships to help him/her recognize the need

to protect him/herself from the partner (e.g., 50% of violent crimes are committed by the victim's partner; one out of three high school and college-aged youth experience abuse at some point in a relationship; battering is the single major cause of injury to women; or abuse rarely occurs once and usually increases in frequency and severity over time).

5. Articulate thoughts, feelings, and a plan that supports terminating the abusive relationship. (11, 12, 13)

11. Explore the student's fears of reprisal from the partner (e.g., threats of physical or sexual or financial harm) and develop a plan of action to respond to these fears (e.g., obtain a court order of protection; change locks, bank accounts, and routes to class/work; have a bag packed and stored in an accessible location and a spare set of car keys hidden for a quick escape; have an emergency money fund; have a friend's name, phone number, and house keys in a safe and accessible location).

12. Explore the student's feelings about the partner or about himself/herself that makes leaving the relationship difficult (e.g., believes the partner really loves him/her; is always very sorry after an abusive episode and promises to never do it again; cries and begs him/her not to leave; does wonderful things immediately after an episode to make up for the abuse; or is really a great person who had a terrible life and just needs someone to love and

understand him/her); reframe these experiences and beliefs with a stronger reality basis.

13. Discuss the partner's responses to the student's attempts to end the relationship (e.g., who else would want or put up with you; it's your fault for making me so angry; where else do you have to go; without me, you will be all alone; I'll find you and kill you if you try to leave; or I'll kill myself if you leave me); emphasize that certain responses are typical and geared to make the student feel guilty or afraid.

6. Verbalize a deeper understanding of the effects of abuse after educating self on the subject. (14, 15)

14. As homework, ask the student to read material that will help him/her understand the effects of abuse (e.g., *The Paper Bag Princess* by Munsch, *Women Who Love Too Much* by Norwood, or *Shame and Guilt: Masters of Disguise* by Middelton-Moz); process the material with the student after it has been read.

15. Encourage the student to participate in a support group for victims of abuse, Al-Anon, or a therapy group where he/she can obtain education as well as the support and companionship of individuals who struggle with similar issues; provide information to him/her about such group opportunities on campus or in the community.

7. Implement physical fitness and stress management behaviors that result in increased verbalizations of personal safety and a sense of self-efficacy. (16, 17)

16. Refer the student to the campus recreation or wellness centers to participate in a self-defense class, yoga, or any program that teaches physical fitness and psychological centering to

increase his/her feelings of self-confidence.

17. Outline stress-management techniques with the student and suggest that he/she select at least two techniques to include daily (e.g., time outs: moments that provide physical comfort and time to reflect; a healthy daily routine that includes sufficient time for sleeping, eating, studying, and socializing; or affirmations posted around the living space).

8. Take action that results in improved academic performance. (18, 19, 20)

18. Review the syllabi for each class in which the student is enrolled and have him/her record any concerns about understanding class material, missing assignments, poor grades, papers due, or attendance.

19. Help the student create a plan of action to improve his/her academic performance (e.g., obtain a tutor at the campus learning assistance center, make appointments with professors to discuss their concerns with his/her performance and elicit their suggestions for improvement, or withdraw from a class if necessary and possible).

20. Assist the student in designing a time-management program that will ensure the completion of all academic work and review his/her program at each session (see the Time Management chapter in this *Planner*).

9. Resume involvement in personal interests and social activities that were sacrificed

21. Encourage the student to make study dates and socialization/recreation dates with friends and

to please the partner.
(21, 22, 23)

classmates; reinforce success
and redirect failure.

22. Explore the student's interest in
campus organizations and
promote his/her involvement.

23. Encourage the student to share
his/her interests and passions
and help him/her identify
campus/community resources
that would welcome his/her
contributions.

10. Increase contact with friends
and family members who will
provide ongoing support.
(24, 25)

24. Explore the student's relationships with friends and family
members, identifying the
individuals who are most likely
to model healthy behaviors in
relationships as well as be
supportive of the student's
efforts to implement positive
relationship behaviors in his/her
own life.

25. Reinforce the student's efforts
to connect with supportive,
affirming individuals by phone,
e-mail, or visits.

11. Verbalize and emulate
behaviors that characterize
healthy relationships.
(26, 27, 28, 29)

26. Discuss the student's positive
relationships with friends and
relatives, asking him/her to pay
particular attention to the
interactions that make him/her
feel safe, capable, and cared for.

27. Suggest that the student begin
to emulate the behaviors and
emotional qualities found in
healthy interactions with potential partners; assist him/her in
listing behaviors that characterize healthy relationships.

28. Encourage the student to read
Dance of Intimacy (Lerner)
and/or *Men, Women and
Relationships: Making Peace*

with the Opposite Sex (Gray); process the material read.

29. Coach the student in maintaining appropriate personal boundaries, improving interpersonal communication skills, and taking responsibility for his/her own happiness.

12. Develop a track record of abuse-free relationships. (30, 31, 32)

30. Meet weekly with the student until there is evidence that his/her relationship with the abusive partner has terminated or substantively changed (e.g., no report of violent behaviors; conflict is managed in healthy ways; or has resumed active involvement in school, work, friendships, and outside interests).

31. If the relationship continues to be unsafe, assist the student in managing the termination process.

32. Meet weekly until the student demonstrates that he/she can set appropriate limits within relationships and will not tolerate a partner or friend who uses abusive tactics.

___. _____   ___. _____
     _____   _____
___. _____   ___. _____
     _____   _____
___. _____   ___. _____
     _____   _____

DIAGNOSTIC SUGGESTIONS:

Axis I:	308.3	Acute Stress Disorder
	300.02	Generalized Anxiety Disorder
	300.00	Anxiety Disorder NOS
	309.xx	Adjustment Disorder
	309.24	Adjustment Disorder with Anxiety
	296.2x	Major Depressive Disorder, Single Episode
	305.00	Alcohol Abuse
	V71.09	No Diagnosis
	799.9	Diagnosis Deferred
	_____	_____
	_____	_____
Axis II:	301.9	Personality Disorder NOS
	V71.09	No Diagnosis
	799.9	Diagnosis Deferred
	_____	_____
	_____	_____

ACADEMIC MAJOR SELECTION

BEHAVIORAL DEFINITIONS

1. Feels unable to clearly define the academic major that would fit with his/her interests, abilities, and world view.
2. Lacks knowledge of the content of various academic disciplines.
3. Lacks the ability to identify avenues that provide specific information on the connection between choice of an academic major and choice of a career.
4. Harbors inaccurate and/or vague information about academic majors and their link to career choices.
5. Parents/family do not approve of the student's choice of major.
6. Making a decision about an academic major feels impossible because of the overwhelming number of choices and amount of information that must be considered.
7. Made a decision about selecting an academic major at an earlier developmental stage and it no longer fits current interests, values, or abilities.
8. Experiences difficulty coping with the ambiguity of having an undeclared major.

—. _____
_____
—. _____
_____
—. _____
_____

LONG-TERM GOALS

1. Select an academic major that will satisfy both personal and career development needs.
2. Collect information about the content and focus of various majors.
3. Increase awareness of the connection between the choice of academic major and values, interests, and skill sets.
4. Increase awareness of the connection between the choice of academic major and career choices.
5. Develop strategies for effectively managing ambiguity while gathering information about academic fields of study.

—. _____

_____

—. _____

_____

—. _____

_____

SHORT-TERM OBJECTIVES

1. Identify the basis for concerns about selecting an academic major. (1, 2, 3, 4)

THERAPEUTIC INTERVENTIONS

1. Explore the student's knowledge base about the content and career paths of various academic disciplines.

2. Discuss the majors that the student has considered to this point and determine the reasons these majors were under consideration.

3. Explore the student's feelings about the study of his/her favored disciplines.

4. Develop a written plan of action to help the student understand the steps that need to be taken when selecting an academic major and the time each step is likely to require.

2. Identify academic majors that have course requirements that seem interesting. (5, 6, 7)

3. Utilize career planning resources and services offered by the campus. (8, 9, 10, 11)

4. Review outcomes of information gathering, testing, course/ workshop participation to

5. Introduce the student to the university's course catalog as a resource for information about the content of various academic majors.

6. Ask the student to review the catalog and identify majors with course requirements that sound interesting and exciting.

7. Explore what interests the student about specific classes and majors.

8. Suggest that the student explore the services of the campus's career center on testing, career planning courses and workshops, and print and online resources.

9. Explain the value of assessment inventories (e.g., Strong Interest Inventory or Myers-Briggs Type Indicator) in helping the student clarify interests, values, skills, and lifestyle preferences; administer him/her for administration of interest inventories and provide feedback on results to the student.

10. Refer the student to courses and workshops that focus on self-assessment and encourage him/ her to register for one of these options.

11. Refer the student to campus clubs and organizations that match the student's academic interests and encourage him/ her to investigate these organizations.

12. Compare and contrast academic disciplines of interest to the student using poster paper; base

shorten the list of academic options. (12, 13)

    comparison on the student's interest in and rigor of course content, ability set required to perform well in each discipline, skill set developed by studying these disciplines, and career options that are typical choices for the disciplines.

13. Ask the student to select two top choices for majors and research these in depth (e.g., talking to senior students who are majoring in these fields, professors in these departments, or people who are working in these career fields).

5. Meet with the campus's key personnel in selected fields of study. (14, 15, 16, 17)

14. Help the student identify and connect with appropriate academic advisors in each discipline.

15. Encourage the student to obtain permission from professors to sit in on several classes in each major.

16. Suggest that the student talk to senior students in each major to obtain their perspectives on the academic fields they selected.

17. Encourage the student to contact the alumni office or career center to locate and speak with alumni from his/her favored disciplines.

6. Create a list of pros and cons for each academic major considered to clarify alternatives. (18, 19)

18. Assist the student in revising the original comparison flip chart of his/her two selected majors developed earlier, based on information collected from course observations and discussions with senior students, alumni, professors, and career professionals.

7. Share decision-making processes with significant others whose input is important to the final outcome. (20)

8. Make a decision about an academic major and live with it for a semester. (21, 22, 23)

9. Declare the academic major. (24)

19. Discuss the outcome of the final comparison with the student to process the factual and affective information gathered; generate a final list of pros and cons for each of the two academic majors of interest.

20. Encourage the student to share the decision-making process and information with parents, family members, and other significant people to keep them informed and obtain their input.

21. Meet with the student for final review of feedback from significant others.

22. Ask the student to choose an academic major, allowing the selected major to guide his/her class selections for the next semester.

23. Meet with the student at the 4th, 8th, and 12th weeks of the following semester to evaluate his/her reaction to the course content and how it fits with his/her interests and abilities.

24. If the student's feelings are positive about the academic major selected, encourage him/her to follow the institution's formal process for declaring a major; if he/she is not satisfied with the major selected, assist the student in considering other academic options.

__. _____   __. _____
     _____   _____
__. _____   __. _____
     _____   _____
__. _____   __. _____
     _____   _____

DIAGNOSTIC SUGGESTIONS:

Axis I: 309.24   Adjustment Disorder with Anxiety
                309.0   Adjustment Disorder with Depressed Mood
                300.3   Obsessive-Compulsive Disorder
                V62.83   Academic Problem
                V65.2   Malingering

                _____   _____
                _____   _____

Axis II: 301.4   Obsessive-Compulsive Personality Disorder
                301.9   Personality Disorder NOS
                V71.09   No Diagnosis

                _____   _____
                _____   _____

ACADEMIC UNDERACHIEVEMENT

BEHAVIORAL DEFINITIONS

1. Has thoughts about assignments and/or tests that provoke feelings of anxiety and prevent optimum academic performance.
2. Expresses fear of failure that leads to avoidance of allocating the necessary time and effort to studying.
3. Is unable or unwilling to employ study skills necessary for academic achievement at the college level (e.g., note-taking in class, underlining and summarizing reading, or test-taking strategies).
4. Demonstrates a decline in academic performance in response to environmental stress (e.g., parents' divorce, death of a loved one, loss of a relationship, or roommate conflict).
5. Maintains unrealistically high expectations for academic achievement.
6. Feels unable to meet family demands for academic performance.
7. Lacks time-management and/or goal-setting skills.
8. Has a learning style that conflicts with the typical instructional methods used by college professors.
9. Has a learning disability that impedes/prevents academic success.
10. Experiences difficulty remaining attentive in lectures and classroom discussions.
11. Attends class and/or participates at a level below that necessary for academic success.
12. Frequently engages in family, work, and social commitments, reducing the amount of time available for academic work to an unacceptable level.

__. _____

_____

__. _____

_____

__. _____

_____

LONG-TERM GOALS

1. Learn and implement stress-management skills to reduce academic performance anxiety.
2. Hone study skills that are necessary for academic achievement in college.
3. Employ the time-management and goal-setting skills necessary for academic success.
4. Develop realistic expectations about academic ability to benchmark academic achievement.
5. Significantly improve class attendance and in-class participation.
6. Identify learning disabilities (if any) and create and implement an educational plan for academic success.
7. Create strategies to effectively manage the expectations of significant others for academic achievement.

—. _____

_____

_____

—. _____

_____

—. _____

_____

SHORT-TERM OBJECTIVES	THERAPEUTIC INTERVENTIONS
1. Clarify the facts, beliefs, and feelings about academic ability and performance and discuss in session. (1, 2, 3)	1. Explore the student's beliefs about his/her academic ability and performance; review his/her history of academic performance (e.g., GPA, grade transcript, or number of classes enrolled in per term).
	2. Identify the key factors that have combined to create the student's beliefs about his/her academic ability and perform-ance (e.g., parental pressure, teachers' feedback, or academic history, personal/career ambitions).

2. Explore the impact of personal belief system on academic behaviors. (4, 5, 6)

3. Help the student identify and clarify feelings (e.g., anxiety, doubt, frustration, guilt, joy, pride, or shame) generated by his/her beliefs about academic ability and performance.

4. Ask the student to list, as specifically as possible, his/her belief statements (or expectations) about his/her academic ability and performance (e.g., "I must get all As" or "I am not going to do well in math anyway, so there is no point to studying").

5. Help the student evaluate each of his/her beliefs about his/her academic performance using the questions, "Is this a reasonable (rational) expectation?" and "Is this an achievable expectation?" as criteria.

6. Assist the student in recognizing the connection between irrational and/or unachievable academic beliefs or expectations and the emotional struggles and academic problems he/she is currently experiencing.

3. Restructure academic expectations, making them rational and conducive to constructive academic behaviors. (7, 8, 9, 10)

7. Assign the student homework of revising his/her belief statements, making each statement more reasonable and achievable (e.g., "I am committed to maintaining a 2.8 to 3.5 GPA each semester" or "I can improve my math performance and will do so by utilizing the learning assistance resources provided on campus").

8. Review the student's belief statements and discuss

similarities to and differences from the original unreasonable statements.

9. Ask the student to identify and record positive emotional reactions and academic behaviors that each revised belief statement would generate.

10. Assign the student homework of creating a plan of action to incorporate and prioritize positive academic behaviors (e.g., "I will use Sunday evenings to review the academic demands of the week ahead and make necessary adjustments to my schedule"; "I will immediately discuss problem grades on homework, tests, and/or papers with my professors"; and "I will seek the assistance of the tutoring center if I am having ongoing difficulty with a particular class") according to his/her current academic needs.

4. Utilize learning assistance resources offered by the campus to improve study skills and habits. (11, 12)

11. Encourage the student to register for courses that teach study skills or to attend workshops or programs that focus on developing reading, listening, note-taking, test-taking, or other effective academic learning strategies.

12. Refer the student to campus-based peer or professional tutors for assistance in understanding specific course content essential to the successful completion of his/her current classes.

5. Analyze time commitments through journaling. (13, 14, 15)

13. Ask the student to list weekly academic, job, social, and

personal commitments and the corresponding amounts of time required to accomplish each one, paying particular attention to class attendance and completion of academic work.

14. Assign a time journal to log all student activities in 30-minute segments for one full week (see Time Management chapter in this *Planner*).

15. Compare the student's original list of time commitments to his/her time journal, asking him/her to identify activities where there are discrepancies between the projected time required by each activity and the actual time spent.

6. Maintain a schedule that encourages academic achievement by successfully balancing academic, work, social, and personal commitments of time and energy. (16, 17)

16. Assist the student in creating a schedule for the next week that reallocates time spent in areas where discrepancies existed to produce a more balanced and productive week (see Time Management chapter in this *Planner*).

17. Encourage the student to use a structured schedule each week to guide his/her time usage and assist in the achievement of academic behaviors outlined in his/her plan of action.

7. Cooperate with an evaluation for the presence of a learning disability. (18)

18. If appropriate, suggest that the student explore the possibility of learning disabilities causing his/her performance deficits and refer him/her for the testing necessary for an accurate diagnosis.

8. Implement a learning plan that incorporates learning style strengths. (19, 20, 21)

19. Suggest that the student investigate various learning styles (e.g., Kolb's Learning Style Inventory, Myers-Briggs Type Indicator, or similar inventories can be used) to determine his/her learning style.

20. Ask the student to work with a learning-assistance counselor to develop an individualized learning plan to identify specific classroom and study behaviors that are most effective with his/her learning style and/or learning disabilities.

21. Incorporate the suggestions from the individualized learning plan into the student's plan of action and review his/her progress at each session to ensure that learning skills are being developed and learning objectives are being met.

9. Demonstrate skills necessary to communicate effectively in writing. (22, 23)

22. Refer the student to the campus's writing clinic and/or peer tutoring center for ongoing assistance with writing assignments.

23. Encourage the student to identify a friend who will act as his/her editor for any assignments that are not reviewed by a tutor.

10. Increase the frequency of verbal participation in the classroom learning process. (24, 25, 26)

24. Contract with the student to speak at least once per class in each course that allows or encourages classroom participation.

25. Suggest that the student become involved in at least one study group where active participation is the norm.

11. Gather the support of significant others by sharing academic expectations, learning plans, and activities. (27, 28)

12. Report a sense of self-efficacy about academic performance. (10, 17, 29)

26. Ask the student to register for a speech or group communications course to demystify the process of and reduce his/her anxiety about speaking in front of others.

27. Assist the student in developing talking points about the changes in his/her academic expectations and behaviors that he/she can use in discussions with significant others, and explore the corresponding impact on the expectations of significant others.

28. Encourage the student to provide significant others with progress updates that will keep them aware of his/her academic struggles and successes.

10. Assign the student homework of creating a plan of action to incorporate and prioritize positive academic behaviors (e.g., "I will use Sunday evenings to review the academic demands of the week ahead and make necessary adjustments to my schedule"; "I will immediately discuss problem grades on homework, tests, and/or papers with my professors"; and "I will seek the assistance of the tutoring center if I am having ongoing difficulty with a particular class") according to his/her current academic needs.

17. Encourage the student to use a structured schedule each week to guide his/her time usage and assist in the achievement of

academic behaviors outlined in his/her plan of action.

29. Review the student's progress on his/her plan of action weekly for the remainder of the semester and biweekly to monthly during the next semester to ensure that new behaviors and skills are operationalized.

13. Identify the debilitating effects of high anxiety levels on academic performance. (30, 31)

30. Teach the student about the debilitating effects of anxiety on academic performance (e.g., increased distractibility, reduced ability to recall material, increased strength of negative outcome expectations, preoccupation with physiological aspects of anxiety [increased heart rate, perspiration, shallow breathing, or dizziness], or fatigue from muscle tension and sleep disturbance).

31. Ask the student to list how he/she perceives anxiety is making a negative impact of his/her academic performance.

14. Identify and address the suspected causes of performance anxiety. (32, 33)

32. Assist the student in identifying the causes of his/her debilitating performance anxiety (e.g., unreasonable personal beliefs or expectations about academic performance, unreasonable expectations from parents, past failure experiences, recent adjustment problems to life on campus, lack of tutorial assistance for new and difficult material, or poor study skills or time management).

33. Develop a plan to address the identified causes of the student's performance anxiety (e.g.,

replace irrational beliefs about academic performance, confront parental expectations directly, apply problem solving to campus life issues of conflict, access campus-based tutoring services, implement effective study skills or time-management procedures).

15. Implement relaxation techniques to reduce test-taking stress. (34, 35, 36)

34. Teach the student relaxation skills (e.g., deep muscle release, deep breathing, or progressive relaxation) to implement at times of high test anxiety or general performance stress.

35. Teach the student the use of positive imagery techniques (e.g., imagining a relaxing scene of laying on a beach under the warm sun, full and clear recall of facts during a test situation, or successful enactment of skills in front of a group) to induce calm, relaxation, and a sense of peace during times of high test or performance anxiety.

36. Use role-playing to help the student apply relaxation and positive imagery skills to specific debilitating perform-ance anxiety situations.

16. Report increased confidence in ability following imple-mentation of effective study skills in preparation for tests. (11, 37, 38)

11. Encourage the student to register for courses that teach study skills or attend workshops or programs that focus on developing reading, listening, note-taking, test-taking, or other effective study strategies.

37. Review the student's imple-mentation of effective study skills; reinforce success and redirect failure.

38. Reassure the student that adequate preparation using effective study methods and prudent time management (see Time Management chapter in this *Planner*) will result in good academic performance as anxiety is reduced.

—. _____   —. _____

   _____   _____

—. _____   —. _____

   _____   _____

—. _____   —. _____

   _____   _____

DIAGNOSTIC SUGGESTIONS:

Axis I:	300.02	Generalized Anxiety Disorder
	300.00	Anxiety Disorder NOS
	309.24	Adjustment Disorder with Anxiety
	314.01	Attention-Deficit/Hyperactivity Disorder, Combined Type
	V62.3	Academic Problem
	799.9	Diagnosis Deferred
	V71.09	No Diagnosis

_____   _____

_____   _____

Axis II:	799.9	Diagnosis Deferred
	V71.09	No Diagnosis

_____   _____

_____   _____

ANTISOCIAL BEHAVIOR

BEHAVIORAL DEFINITIONS

1. Has a history of frequent rule breaking, lying, physical aggression, showing disrespect for others and their property, stealing, and/or substance abuse that has resulted in frequent confrontation with authority figures (e.g., parents, law enforcement, or school officials).
2. Consistently blames others for what happens to him/her.
3. Refuses to follow rules of the dorm, campus, university, and/or society, with the attitude that they apply others, not him/her.
4. Has a history of frequent reckless behaviors that reflects a lack of regard for the safety of self or others and shows a high need for excitement beyond the norm of having fun.
5. Consistently lies to get around requirements, mitigate rule violations, and avoid consequences of his/her actions.
6. Has never been totally monogamous in any relationship for a period of a year, using sexuality to take advantage of or manipulate others.
7. Demonstrates a pattern of interacting in an irritable, aggressive, and/or argumentative way with roommates, classroom peers, faculty, parents, university administrators, and others.
8. Shows little or no remorse for hurtful behavior to others, perhaps voicing insincere regret if the student believes that it will mitigate any negative consequences.
9. Often initiates physical fighting with roommates, classmates, faculty, or others.
10. Repeatedly has performed antisocial acts that may or may not have led to arrests or suspensions from school (e.g., destroying property, stealing, drug dealing, dealing in stolen property, using roommates' belongings without permission to do so, or cheating on examinations).
11. Engages in impulsive behaviors, such as frequently changing dorms or roommates; moving often; traveling with no goal; or changing major, classes, or universities without forethought.

12. Does not attend classes regularly or fails to fulfill course requirements in a timely fashion.

__. _____

_____

__. _____

_____

__. _____

_____

LONG-TERM GOALS

1. Keep behavior within acceptable limits of university rules in particular, and society, in general.
2. Develop and demonstrate a healthy sense of respect for social mores, university rules, campus expectations, rights of others, and the need for honesty in dealing with others.
3. Demonstrate respect for university authority figures and faculty.
4. Relate to roommates and classmates with more respect, less defensiveness, more sensitivity, and less intimidation.
5. Come to an understanding and acceptance of the need for limits and boundaries for one's own behavior.
6. Except responsibility for one's actions, including sincerely apologizing for past hurts and transgressions, not blaming others and complying with rules and accepting consequences.
7. Maintain consistent class attendance and demonstrate academic responsibility by making satisfactory progress in course work.

__. _____

_____

__. _____

_____

__. _____

_____

SHORT-TERM OBJECTIVES	THERAPEUTIC INTERVENTIONS
1. Admit to illegal, unethical, and/or inappropriate behavior that violated campus expectations, university rules, the law and/or rights and feelings of roommates, classmates, and/or faculty. (1, 2, 3)	1. Actively build a level of trust with the student in individual sessions using consistent eye contact, active listening, unconditional positive regard, and warm acceptance of the student to help increase his/her ability to identify and express feelings.
	2. Explore the history of the student's pattern of illegal and/or unethical behaviors and confront his/her attempts at minimalization, denial, mitigation, or projection of blame to others, the situation, or circumstance.
	3. Review the consequences of the student's antisocial behaviors for the student and roommates, classmates, faculty, and/or parents.
2. Verbalize an understanding of the benefits to self and others of treating others with respect and earning their trust. (4, 5)	4. Teach the student that the basis for all relationships is trust and that individuals should treat one another with respect and kindness.
	5. Teach the student the need to comply with campus rules, mores, social expectations, and societal laws as the basis for trust, avoiding anarchy in the society as a whole as well as providing personal advantage.
3. Make a commitment to live within the rules and regulations of the campus, university, and laws of society. (5, 6)	5. Teach the student the need to comply with campus rules, mores, social expectations, and societal laws as the basis for trust, avoiding anarchy in the

society as a whole as well as providing personal advantage.

6. Solicit a commitment from the student to live in a prosocial, law-abiding, university-rule-compliant lifestyle.

4. Implement assertiveness and problem-solving strategies in place of aggressive or manipulative behavior. (7, 8, 9)

7. Introduce the student to a model for assertive actions that respectfully identifies issues in behavioral terms, recognizes both individuals' needs and rights, and offers possible solutions that are mutually beneficial in lieu of manipulative, aggressive, or antisocial methods.

8. Teach the student effective conflict resolution or problem-solving skills: (a) problem identification or clarification in behavioral terms; (b) mutual brainstorming of possible alternative solutions and review of the pros and cons of each; (c) mutual selection of an alternative solution for implementation; (d) evaluation of the outcome in terms of mutual satisfaction; and (e) adjustment of the solution, if necessary, to increase mutual satisfaction.

9. Use role-play and modeling to teach the student the application of effective conflict resolution techniques to his/her daily activities on campus and in interactions with roommates, classmates, faculty, parents, and others.

5. Identify and replace distorted self-talk that precipitates

10. Assist the student in identifying his/her negative, distorted self-

inappropriate, antisocial
behavior(s). (10, 11)

talk that precipitates or mediates
antisocial actions (e.g., "It's
much easier to just act like I'm
going along with this, but I'll
back out when the time comes"
or "I can get away with anything
with these professors/classmates
and they'll never know it").

11. Teach the student realistic,
positive self-talk to increase
his/her sense of peace and
fairness in negotiating
relationships with others (e.g.,
"It builds trust when I'm
honest," "If I follow through
with my commitments my
grades will show it," or "I can
act like the reasonable and
intelligent person I am").

6. Identify and replace irrational
beliefs that spur inappropriate,
antisocial behavior(s). (12, 13)

12. Assist the student in identifying
his/her irrational beliefs that act
as barriers to appropriate social
interactions (e.g., "It's dog eat
dog here, so I need to do
whatever it takes to have the
advantage" or "You can't trust
anyone, so why should I be
honest?").

13. Teach the student to rationally
reframe his/her irrational beliefs
to remove barriers to appropriate
social functioning on campus
and elsewhere (e.g., "Most
people are truthful and you can
believe what they tell you," "No
one is out to get an advantage
over me," or "Learning to trust
others is the beginning of
friendship").

7. Acknowledge a pattern of self-
centeredness in past and/or
current relationships and
interactions with family,

14. Review the student's relationships that have been lost because
of his/her antisocial attitudes
and practices (e.g., disloyalty,

roommates, classmates, and/or others. (14, 15)

dishonesty, aggression, or manipulation).

15. Confront the student's lack of sensitivity to the needs and feelings of roommates, class-mates, faculty, parents, and others; use role-reversal or empty-chair techniques to increase the student's awareness of the feelings of others and the negative impact of his/her callousness.

8. List the consequences of continued antisocial behavior practices. (16)

16. Emphasize to the student the seriousness of the negative consequences (e.g., arrests, incarceration, loss of friends, suspension from school, or loss of respect from self and others) if he/she continues to disrespect the rules of society and authority figures who impose and enforce them.

9. Make a commitment to be consistently honest and reliable in relationships with room-mates, classmates, faculty, and parents. (17, 18)

17. Teach the student the value of honesty and reliability as the basis for trust and respect in relationships with roommates, classmates, faculty, parents, and others when they are not disappointed or hurt by lies and broken promises; assign him/her to list the benefits of honesty for himself/herself and others.

18. Ask the student to make a commitment to be honest and reliable with others; role-play and use role-reversal techniques to teach the implementation of honesty in interactions with others.

10. Verbalize an understanding of the benefits to self and others

15. Confront the student's lack of sensitivity to the needs and

of being empathic and sensitive to the needs of roommates, classmates, faculty, parents, and others. (15, 19)

11. List three actions that will be performed as acts of kindness and thoughtfulness toward roommates, classmates, faculty, parents, and others. (20)

12. Make amends or restitution for the hurt caused to roommates, classmates, faculty, parents, and others by past behaviors and actions. (21, 22, 23)

13. Attend classes consistently and reliability, comply with

feelings of roommates, classmates, faculty, parents, and others; use role-reversal or empty-chair techniques to increase the student's awareness of the feelings of others and the negative impact of his/her callousness.

19. Confront the student for incidents of being rude, unkind, or disrespectful of roommates, classmates, faculty, parents, and others; for each incident, ask him/her to describe an alternate kind and sensitive reaction.

20. Assist the student to list three actions that he/she will perform as acts of service or kindness for others; follow up in subsequent sessions what happened and what was learned.

21. Assist the student in identifying those having been hurt by his/her antisocial behaviors.

22. Teach the student the value of apologizing for past hurts caused by his/her actions as a means of accepting responsibility for his/her behavior and in developing sensitivity to the feelings of others.

23. Encourage a commitment to specific steps that will be taken to apologize and/or make restitution to those who have suffered from the student's past hurtful behaviors; follow up on the implementation of these steps, reinforcing success and redirecting failure.

24. Review the rules and expectations that must govern behavior

campus rules, and treat faculty and classmates with respect and courtesy. (24, 25)

at the academic/campus setting; ask the student to comply with these rules and assist him/her in listing the benefits of compliance (e.g., continued student status, future graduation, or letters of recommendation).

25. Monitor the student's attendance, behavior, and performance in classes and reinforce reliability as well as respect for the faculty.

14. Identify and implement behaviors that must change to improve relationships with others, especially roommates. (26, 27, 28)

26. Ask the student to make a list of behaviors and attitudes that must be modified to decrease his/her conflict with others (especially roommates); process the list in session.

27. Assist the student in listing the behaviors that are required to be a responsible, nurturing, consistently reliable roommate and friend (e.g., honesty, reliability, sensitivity, empathy, or kindness).

28. Develop a plan with the student to begin to implement specific actions as a responsible individual (focus on reality-based activities); review the implementation, reinforce success, and redirect failure.

15. Increase statements accepting full responsibility for own behavior, thoughts, and feelings. (29, 30, 31)

29. Confront the student when he/she makes blaming statements or fails to take responsibility for negative actions, thoughts, or feelings toward others.

30. Explore the student's reasons for blaming others for his/her own actions and respond with reality-based feedback and perspective.

16. Verbalize an understanding of how childhood experiences of pain and aggression have led to an imitative pattern of self-focused protection and aggression toward others. (32, 33)

31. Give verbal positive feedback to the student when he/she takes responsibility for his/her own behaviors; process and compare the difference with former ways of responding.

32. Explore any history of abuse, neglect, or abandonment in the student's childhood.

33. Point out to the student how a pattern of emotional detachment in relationships and self-focused behavior are dysfunctional attempts to protect himself/herself from an expectation of pain.

17. Verbalize a desire to forgive perpetrator(s) of childhood abuse. (34)

34. Teach the value of forgiveness of the perpetrator(s) of hurt versus holding on to hurt and rage as an excuse to continue antisocial practices; recommend that the student read material on the value of the process of forgiveness (e.g., *Forgive and Forget* by Smedes, *Healing the Shame* by Bradshaw).

18. Verbalize fears associated with trusting others. (35)

35. Explore fears the student has that are associated with placing trust in roommates, classmates, faculty, parents, and others.

19. Demonstrate trust in a significant other, parents, roommates, and/or the counselor by disclosure of personal feelings. (36, 37)

36. Identify the student's personal thoughts and feelings that he/she can share with a significant other or roommates to begin to demonstrate trust in someone; assign him/her to share at least one time per day during the next week.

37. Process the student's experiences of making himself/herself vulnerable by self-disclosing to roommates, classmates, faculty, parents, and others.

__._ _____ __._ _____
_____ _____

__._ _____ __._ _____
_____ _____

__._ _____ __._ _____
_____ _____

DIAGNOSTIC SUGGESTIONS:

Axis I:	309.3	Adjustment Disorder with Disturbance of Conduct
	312.8	Conduct Disorder
	312.34	Intermittent Explosive Disorder
	303.90	Alcohol Dependence
	304.20	Cocaine Dependence
	304.89	Polysubstance Dependence
	_____	_____
	_____	_____
Axis II:	301.7	Antisocial Personality Disorder
	301.81	Narcissistic Personality Disorder
	799.9	Diagnosis Deferred
	V71.09	No Diagnosis
	_____	_____
	_____	_____

CAREER CHOICE CONFUSION

BEHAVIORAL DEFINITIONS

1. Is unable to identify careers that fit with values, interests, skills, worldview.
2. Feels confused, anxious, or depressed when thinking about career choice.
3. Lacks information about or experience in various occupations.
4. Bases opinions about careers on vague and/or inaccurate information.
5. Lacks knowledge of research avenues that provide occupational information.
6. Is unable to connect the knowledge and skills developed through the study of an academic major to the requirements of a career.
7. Made a decision about a career at an earlier developmental point and it no longer fits current values, interests, skills.
8. Experiences anxiety because of the ambiguity that exists during career decision-making process.
9. Views the career decision-making process as overwhelming because of the amount of self-assessment and world-of-work information that must be collected, analyzed, and synthesized.
10. Avoids accepting the responsibilities of adulthood by delaying career choices.
11. Parents/family do not approve of the student's career interests.

—. _____
   _____
—. _____
   _____
—. _____
   _____

LONG-TERM GOALS

1. Embrace a career that will fit personal characteristics, professional goals, and lifestyle choices.
2. Increase awareness of connection between personal traits, values, and skills and career satisfaction.
3. Understand the role of an academic major in assisting in the career-choice process.
4. Gather information about options within the career fields of interest.
5. Participate in opportunities to gain experience in various careers.
6. Develop strategies to effectively manage the expectations of significant others about career selection.
7. Develop strategies to effectively cope with emotions elicited by the ambiguity of the career-choice process.

—. _____

_____

—. _____

_____

—. _____

_____

SHORT-TERM OBJECTIVES	THERAPEUTIC INTERVENTIONS
1. Identify specific thoughts and feelings about choosing a career. (1, 2)	1. Explore the student's level of interest in and knowledge of specific career areas.
	2. Explore the student's feelings about career choice and acknowledge the difficulty of this decision-making process.
2. Identify personal characteristics and external factors that influence career path decisions. (3, 4)	3. Identify key factors that have influenced the student's ideas about careers (e.g., childhood experiences, parental pressure, important role model, media exposure, financial goals, or academic coursework).
	4. Assess the student's ability to articulate his/her personal

3. Utilize career decision-making resources offered by the campus. (5, 6, 7)

4. Review outcomes of information gathering and course/workshop participation to develop a list of the five most preferred career options. (8, 9)

5. Research detailed information about the most preferred career options. (10, 11)

characteristics (e.g., values, traits, interests, or skills) and understand their connection to his/her career choice.

5. Suggest that the student explore the services of the campus's career center for the availability of testing, career planning workshops, and print and online resources.

6. Explain the value of assessment inventories (e.g., Strong Interest Inventory or Myers-Briggs Type Indicator) in helping the student clarify interests, values, skills, and lifestyle preferences; administer or refer him/her for administration of interest inventories and provide feedback on results.

7. Refer the student to courses and workshops that focus on self-assessment and encourage him/her to register for one of these options.

8. Assist the student in developing a chart to compare and contrast careers of interest; list such things as the skill set needed for competency in each career, values inherent in each career, environments typical for each career, lifestyle each career lends itself to, and worldview created by each career.

9. Ask the student to select his/her top five possible career choices and make a commitment to research these in depth.

10. Encourage the student to conduct an online search for web sites that provide information on selected careers.

6. Share the career-choice process with significant others whose input is important to the final outcome. (12)

7. Develop a list of individuals who have experience in the preferred careers to contact and obtain information. (13, 14, 15)

8. Conduct information interviews with professionals who have experience in the careers being considered. (16, 17, 18)

11. Suggest that the student use the resources of the career services center and/or university library to find books and video information on selected careers.

12. Encourage the student to share his/her career-choice process with parents, family members, and significant others to keep them informed of the process and solicit their feedback.

13. Refer the student to the alumni office and/or the career services office to participate in available networking and/or mentoring programs related to his/her preferred career options.

14. Ask the student to get in touch with professional associations related to his/her selected career to gather more information and identify possible professional contacts.

15. Assist the student in creating a list of networking possibilities related to his/her preferred career options, using family, friends, and faculty as resources.

16. As homework, ask the student to create or obtain a list of interviewing questions to gather information from those who have experience in his/her preferred career options.

17. Role-play an information-gathering interview, helping the student refine his/her questions and become comfortable with the interviewing process.

9. Create a pro-and-con list for each career under consideration to identify the top two options. (19, 20)

18. Assign the student homework of conducting two information-gathering interviews for each career of interest.

19. Assist the student in revising the original comparison chart of careers based on information collected from networking discussions and information interviews.

20. Discuss the outcome of the comparison with the student to process all the factual and affective information gathered; generate a list of pros and cons for each of the careers of interest, narrowing the preferred list to two options.

10. Participate in at least one experiential work opportunity on campus or in the community for each of the careers under consideration. (21, 22)

21. Assist the student in identifying campus resources for experiential career opportunities (e.g., internships, fieldwork, community service, volunteer options, or season or part time employment).

22. Encourage the student to contact individuals on his/her networking list that may provide a contact or connection to an internship or other work experience.

11. Using information gained from the experiential involvement, reevaluate top career options. (23, 24)

23. Meet with the student monthly during the internship period to evaluate his/her experience and fine-tune his/her career choice.

24. Return to the pros and cons list for each of the careers, adding information gained from direct experience and identify the career that is the best fit.

12. Choose a career and create a postgraduation plan of action. (25, 26, 27)

25. Assist the student in reviewing the educational requirements of his/her selected profession.

26. Help the student create a plan for researching and applying to graduate or professional school programs, if more education is required.

27. Refer the student to the career services center for assistance with resume writing, interviewing, and job search, if an employment search is beginning.

__. _____

_____

__. _____

_____

__. _____

_____

__. _____

_____

__. _____

_____

__. _____

_____

DIAGNOSTIC SUGGESTIONS:

Axis I:	309.0	Adjustment Disorder with Depressed Mood
	309.24	Adjustment Disorder with Anxiety
	309.28	Adjustment Disorder with Mixed Anxiety and Depressed Mood
	300.4	Dysthymic Disorder
	V62.2	Occupational Problem
	V62.89	Phase of Life Problem
	799.9	Diagnosis Deferred
	V71.09	No Diagnosis
	_____	_____
	_____	_____
Axis II:	799.9	Diagnosis Deferred
	V71.09	No Diagnosis
	_____	_____
	_____	_____

CHEMICAL DEPENDENCE/ABUSE

BEHAVIORAL DEFINITIONS

1. Uses mood-altering substances regularly until high or intoxicated.
2. Has become intoxicated or high on drugs on two or more occasions on campus in the past two months.
3. Has been reported to possess drug paraphernalia, alcohol, and/or illicit substances.
4. Has a history of arrest for alcohol or drug-related charges (e.g., drunk and disorderly, public intoxication, driving while under the influence, or underage drinking).
5. Has changed peer group to one that is noticeably chemically oriented.
6. Demonstrates a decline in school and academic performance and productivity.
7. Experiences frequent mood swings.
8. Is regularly absent from or tardy to classes.
9. Is subject to disciplinary action at school related to substance abuse.
10. Has had a positive drug toxicology finding.

___. _____

_____

___. _____

_____

___. _____

_____

LONG-TERM GOALS

1. Terminate abusive pattern of use of mood-altering substances.
2. Acknowledge a chemical dependence problem while remaining clean and sober and involved in an active recovery program.
3. Develop an understanding of the relapse pattern and strategies for effectively complying to sustained, long-term recovery.
4. Establish and maintain relationships with individuals and groups that support and enhance ongoing recovery.
5. Demonstrate consistent ability to use effective adaptive means to cope with academic, social, and personal stressors that previously fostered substance use or abuse.

—. _____

   _____

—. _____

   _____

—. _____

   _____

SHORT-TERM OBJECTIVES

1. Provide a detailed history of substance use, both before coming to college and since. (1, 2, 3)

THERAPEUTIC INTERVENTIONS

1. Actively build a level of trust with the student using consistent eye contact, active listening, unconditional positive regard, and warm acceptance to increase his/her ability to identify and express feelings that lead to substance use.

2. Collect information on the student's drugs of choice; route of drug intake (e.g., IV, PO, nasal); frequency, amount, and duration of use; most recent use; any physical complaints/medical problems; and negative life consequences (e.g., academic, social, legal, familial, and/or vocational)

resulting from his/her substance abuse.

3. Administer an appropriate substance abuse evaluation instrument (e.g., Alcohol Severity Index or Michigan Alcohol Screening Test) to assess the student's depth and severity of chemical dependence; process results.

2. Tell the complete story of "My reasons for using alcohol and/or drugs." (4, 5)

4. Help the student clarify the reasons for his/her substance use (e.g., emotional and behavioral responses to use of drugs/alcohol) as well as feelings, events, and stressors that trigger substance use/abuse.

5. Ask the student to assess whether his/her substance abuse consistently succeeds at fulfilling each of the reasons for which he/she uses; point out that long-term negative consequences far outweigh any short-term payoffs for substance abuse.

3. Describe the history of alcohol or drug use/abuse by immediate and/or extended family members and its impact. (6, 7, 8)

6. Explore the student's family history for chemical dependence patterns and relate these to his/her current situation.

7. Explore the student's extended family chemical dependence and relate this to a genetic vulnerability for him/her to develop chemical dependence also.

8. Explore the impact of family substance abuse on the student during childhood and in the present; probe for abuse, neglect, or abandonment issues.

4. Make verbal "I" statements to reflect acknowledgment of

9. Assign the student homework of completing an Alcoholics

acceptance of responsibility for and powerlessness over substance use. (9, 10)

Anonymous First Step paper and processing the paper with either a support group, his/her sponsor, or with the therapist to receive feedback.

10. Confront attempts by the student to minimize or deny the seriousness of his/her substance abuse problem.

5. Obtain a medical examination to evaluate the effects of chemical or alcohol use and/or nutritional deficits. (11)

11. Refer the student for a thorough physical examination to determine any negative physical health effects of his/her substance abuse.

6. Identify the negative consequences of drug and/or alcohol use/abuse. (12, 13, 14)

12. Assign the student homework of listing the negative consequences of his/her substance abuse (e.g., academic, health, financial, legal, relationships, self-esteem, employment, productivity, or energy).

13. Assist the student in listing the negative effects his/her substance abuse has had on roommates, classmates, faculty, and/or familial relationships; encourage a plan to make amends for past hurts.

14. Request that the student attend didactic lectures on chemical dependence, its consequences, and the process of recovery; ask him/her to identify, in writing, several key points obtained from each lecture for further processing in subsequent sessions.

7. Verbalize increased knowledge of alcoholism, drug abuse, and/or addiction, in the process of recovery. (14, 15)

14. Request that the student attend didactic lectures on chemical dependence, its consequences, and the process of recovery; ask him/her to identify, in writing, several key points obtained from

each lecture for further processing in subsequent sessions.

15. Assign the student homework of reading information on the disease concept of alcoholism (e.g., *I'll Quit Tomorrow* by Johnson, *The Addiction Workbook* by Fanning and O'Neill) and selecting several key ideas to discuss with the therapist.

8. Attend appropriate self-help groups and contact supportive or sponsoring individuals. (16, 17)

16. Facilitate the student's linkages with appropriate community support groups (e.g., Alcoholics Anonymous, Cocaine Anonymous, or Narcotics Anonymous); verify attendance and process the experience.

17. Direct the student to meet with an Alcoholics Anonymous or Narcotics Anonymous member who has been working the 12-Step program for several years and find out specifically how the program helped him/her stay sober; process the meeting experience.

9. Identify and replace distorted self-talk that precipitates or stimulates drug and/or alcohol use. (18, 19, 20, 21)

18. Assist the student in identifying his/her negative, distorted self-talk that precipitates or mediates feelings to drink or use (e.g., "One more drink, what would that hurt?" or "I know I can stop after one drink, no problem").

19. Teach the student realistic, positive self-talk to increase his/her sense of control over substance addiction (e.g., "I can say no to a true friend and not worry about our friendship" or "I'm not going to trash my hard work for one joint").

20. Assist the student in identifying his/her irrational beliefs that act as barriers to sobriety (e.g., "Everyone drinks, what's the big deal?" or "I don't drink all that much").

21. Teach the student to rationally reframe his/her irrational beliefs to remove barriers to attaining or maintaining sobriety (e.g., "I know that there is a high risk for me that one drink will lead to another, and another, and that's not worth it" or "I now know that drinking is not something that I want to risk my academic career over").

10. Implement relaxation techniques during times of the desire to use drugs and/or alcohol. (22, 23)

22. Teach the student relaxation methods (e.g., progressive muscle relaxation, deep breathing, or guided visual imagery) to deal better with stressful situations; encourage the use of these techniques when tempted to relapse into substance abuse because of feeling tense, nervous, or uptight.

23. Assist the student in listing at least five situations in which relaxation exercises would be a beneficial coping skill (e.g., to reduce tension, induce sleep, cope with test anxiety, reduce social anxiety, or dissipate an urge to use substances).

11. Make a list of recreational, extracurricular, academic, and social activities (and places) that will replace substance-abuse-related activities and venues. (24, 25)

24. Aid the student in exploring positive, appropriate leisure, social, and extracurricular activities as alternatives to idle time, which triggers substance abuse.

25. Help the student to plan campus-related projects and activities that can be accomplished to build self-esteem now that sobriety affords time and energy for such constructive activities.

12. Identify the ways that sobriety positively impacts academic performance and extra curricular activities. (26)

26. Ask the student to make a list reviewing how being sober/drug-free will positively impact his/her grades, college life, social and familial relationships, and/or athletic and extra-curricular experiences.

13. State changes that will be made in social relationships to support recovery. (27, 28)

27. Review the negative influence of the student continuing old alcohol-related or drug-related friendships; ask him/her to identify those relationships that are high risk as relapse triggers and need to be avoided.

28. Assist the student in identifying ways that he/she can develop a positive support system of sober friendships and discuss ways to maintain and reinforce such a positive support system.

14. Implement assertiveness and problem-solving skills to resolve interpersonal stress. (29, 30, 31)

29. Introduce the student to a model for assertive dialog that respectfully identifies issues in behavioral terms, recognizes both individuals' needs and rights, and offers possible solutions that are mutually beneficial not to fall prey to peer pressure to use.

30. Teach the student effective conflict-resolution or problem-solving skills: (a) problem identification or clarification in behavioral terms; (b) mutual brainstorming of possible alternative solutions and review

of the pros and cons of each; (c) mutual selection of an alternative solution for implementation; (d) evaluation of the outcome in terms of mutual satisfaction; and (e) adjustment of the solution, if necessary, to increase mutual satisfaction.

31. Use role-play and modeling to teach the student the application of effective assertiveness techniques to avoid being pressed into substance use by peers.

15. Family and significant others verbalize an understanding of the student's chemical dependence problem and their offer of genuine support for recovery. (32)

32. Meet with family and significant others (after consent is obtained) to educate them about the student's chemical dependence problem, enlist their support, and terminate any enabling patterns.

16. Implement behavioral coping strategies to deal with fears related to maintaining sobriety. (33, 34)

33. Assign the student homework of listing his/her fears associated with being sober and/or drug free.

34. Assist the student in developing a behavioral coping plan for each fear that is associated with maintaining sobriety (e.g., learning social skills, initiating social contact to build a support network of drug-free friends, or making contact with a spiritual support group).

17. Implement specific coping responses to feelings or situations that trigger relapse into drug and/or alcohol use. (22, 31, 35, 36, 37)

22. Teach the student relaxation methods (e.g., progressive muscle relaxation, deep breathing, or guided visual imagery) to deal better with stressful situations; encourage the use of these techniques when tempted to relapse into substance abuse because of

feeling tense, nervous, or uptight.

31. Use role-play and modeling to teach the application of effective assertiveness techniques to avoid being pressed into substance use by peers.

35. Assist the student in identifying and listing his/her typical behavioral responses to being tempted to use again.

36. Review coping responses to overcome the urge to use (e.g., positive self-talk, call a sponsor, attend a self-help group meeting, relaxation procedures, prayer and meditation, assertiveness skills, or prosocial activity diversions).

37. Investigate situational stressors of campus life, academic expectations, and/or extra-curriculars that may foster the student's substance abuse; suggest behavioral or cognitive coping skills to deal with each stressor.

18. Identify a support system in the residence-hall environment that will encourage and assist with maintaining sobriety. (38, 39)

38. Explore administrative staff support (e.g., resident advisor, residence director) with the student that is available to provide him/her suggestions and help to stay clean and sober.

39. Explore the residence hall peer resources (e.g., clean-and-sober peer support group, drug-free dorm and campus-based social activities, spiritually based functions, or 12-Step activities) with the student that are available to him/her in helping to stay clean and sober.

19. Develop a written aftercare plan that will support the maintenance of long-term sobriety during breaks from school and postgraduation. (40)

40. Assign and review the student's written aftercare plan to ensure it is adequate to maintain sobriety (e.g., attendance at Alcoholic Anonymous (AA)/Narcotics Anonymous (NA) meetings, ongoing counseling, positive support network, trigger coping skills to be used, sponsor selected, telephone numbers of supportive people, or spiritual support).

20. Sign an abstinence contract and verbalize and process feelings of fear, grief, and/or reluctance associated with signing the contract. (41)

41. Develop an abstinence contract with the student on the use of his/her drug of choice; process the emotional impact of signing this contract.

__. _____

__. _____

__. _____

__. _____

__. _____

__. _____

DIAGNOSTIC SUGGESTIONS:

Axis I:		
	304.89	Polysubstance Dependence
	303.90	Alcohol Dependence
	305.00	Alcohol Abuse
	304.30	Cannabis Dependence
	305.20	Cannabis Abuse
	304.20	Cocaine Dependence
	305.60	Cocaine Abuse
	304.50	Hallucinogen Dependence
	305.30	Hallucinogen Abuse
	304.60	Inhalant Dependence
	305.90	Inhalant Abuse
	304.10	Sedative, Hypnotic, or Anxiolytic Dependence
	313.81	Oppositional Defiant Disorder

300.4   Dysthymic Disorder
300.02   Generalized Anxiety Disorder
300.23   Social Phobia

————   ————————————————
————   ————————————————

Axis II: 301.7   Antisocial Personality Disorder
               799.9   Diagnosis Deferred
               V71.09   No Diagnosis

————   ————————————————
————   ————————————————

CHILDHOOD ABUSE

BEHAVIORAL DEFINITIONS

1. Presents as depressed and detached with severe mood swings.
2. Avoids or has difficulty maintaining positive, healthy relationships.
3. Displays self-destructive behaviors (e.g., self-mutilation, suicidal behaviors, abusive relationships, or substance abuse).
4. Is unable to complete coursework, maintain employment, or interact with family members due to conflict with authority figures.
5. Is unable to identify and/or discuss feelings (e.g., powerlessness, rage, guilt, fear, shame, or guilt).
6. Does not effectively manage impulsivity (e.g., shopping, eating, or aggressive behavior toward others).
7. Lacks trust and is hypervigilant about environmental cues (e.g., avoids sitting with his or her back to the door, allows no physical contact, or avoids conflict).
8. Is hyperaware of the needs/desires of others even when personal needs go unrecognized/unmet.
9. Experiences sexual dysfunction and/or engages in promiscuity.
10. Complains of chronic physical problems (e.g., back pain, headaches, or nausea).

___. _____

_____

___. _____

_____

___. _____

_____

LONG-TERM GOALS

1. Resolve past childhood/family issues, leading to less anger and depression and greater self-esteem, security, and confidence.
2. Manage emotions constructively to feel more hopeful and empowered.
3. Develop the communication skills necessary to identify and negotiate personal needs as well as to build healthy social and intimate relationships.
4. Replace self-destructive behaviors with healthier coping strategies.
5. Embrace the physical and sexual parts of the self to raise self-esteem and enhance body image.
6. Create a life view that recognizes the impact of the abuse while integrating it into a larger sense of identity and purpose.

—. _____
   _____
—. _____
   _____
—. _____
   _____

SHORT-TERM OBJECTIVES

1. Verbalize a sense of safety within the counseling environment. (1, 2, 3)

THERAPEUTIC INTERVENTIONS

1. Reassure the student that you want to do everything possible to help him/her feel safe and secure.
2. Keep items in the office that offer a sense of comfort (e.g., pillows, a quilt, or stuffed animals) and encourage the student to use them to feel more secure.
3. Offer information about the parameters of therapy and answer any questions the student may have about therapeutic orientation and/or style, paying particular attention to confidentiality concerns.

2. Verbalize a commitment to and an understanding of the counseling process. (4, 5, 6)

4. Encourage the student to choose a weekly appointment day and time that will be his/her standing appointment.

5. Provide the student with emergency contact information to ensure that, if a crisis occurs, he/she will have the option to make a safe connection.

6. Assure the student that, while you will ask questions about important topics related to his/her abuse, he/she can decide what and how much to discuss in sessions.

3. Share as much information as possible about the abuse and its effects. (7, 8)

7. Ask the student to share as much information as he/she is able about the abuse (e.g., form of abuse, individuals involved, or age when abuse began and ended).

8. Validate the student's experiences as abuse and provide him/her with some definitions (*physical abuse:* hitting, biting, punching, or shoving that results in external or internal injuries; *sexual abuse:* sexual contact including oral, anal, and vaginal sex, or digital penetration or penetration with a foreign object for the purpose of sexual gratification; also, fondling, masturbation, seductive behavior, and exposure; *emotional abuse:* verbal assault, lack of verbal or physical affection, and general lack of positive attention).

4. Read material on abuse recovery and attend a support group to learn to normalize feelings and cope more adaptively. (9, 10)

9. As homework, ask the student to read material on recovering from childhood abuse (e.g., *Healing the Shame That Binds*

You by Bradshaw, *Forgiveness: How to Make Peace with Your Past and Get on with Your Life* by Simon and Simon, or *Outgrowing the Pain* by Gil) to understand what constitutes abuse and the impact that abuse has had on his/her life.

10. Refer the student to a support group for adult survivors of childhood abuse and ask him/her to make an initial commitment to attend weekly meetings throughout the semester.

5. Identify current and historical attitudes toward and feelings about the abuse.
   (11, 12, 13, 14)

11. Gently explore the student's statements of denial and belief in myths about abuse (e.g., "It wasn't that bad," "It doesn't affect me now," "It was my fault; I should have stopped it," "I deserved it," or "There must be something wrong with me for _____ to do something like that"); reframe them or expose the myths (e.g., "No child ever deserves to be abused," "No child is ever responsible for the abusive actions of adults," "You did not make this happen," or "You were too small to stop an adult").

12. Assist the student in naming feelings experienced because of the abuse (e.g., shame, guilt, fear, rage, betrayal, powerlessness, abandonment, or sadness) and encourage him/her to describe the situations in which these feelings occurred.

13. Encourage the student to use words, drawings, and/or pictures to journal past and present situations, behaviors, and

feelings that are related to memories of the abuse; process the journal material.

14. Suggest that the student bring pictures of himself/herself at the age of the onset of the abuse (or find pictures in a magazine or book of a child of about that age) to feel sadness and empathy for the child he/she was as well as become more connected to feelings and experiences.

6. Acknowledge the effects of abuse on psychosocial development. (15, 16, 17, 18)

15. Assist the student in identifying the maladaptive coping behaviors he/she developed in childhood (e.g., denial, minimizing, rationalizing, dissociation, cutting, addiction, or isolation), recognizing that these behaviors kept him/her alive and protected him/her emotionally.

16. Gently confront the student with his/her current maladaptive behaviors that are a result of the abuse (e.g., poor or no decision making, inability to set appropriate physical and emotional boundaries, sexual promiscuity, substance abuse, "live fast, die young" life view, or skewed body image).

17. Ask the student to read *Growing Up Again* (Clarke and Dawson) to clarify necessary developmental tasks (of particular interest are tasks related to self-soothing and providing nurture and comfort as well as tasks related to rules and structures inherent in school and work).

18. Assist the student in identifying the specific developmental tasks that were interrupted by the abuse using material from *Growing Up Again* (Clarke and Dawson) or Erikson's stages of psychosocial development, and develop plans to incorporate these tasks into his/her life now (e.g., a therapeutic massage is useful if the Stage 1 task of accepting touch was never accomplished; or trying a completely new activity or type of food is useful if the Stage 2 task of exploring and experiencing the environment was never accomplished).

7. Implement techniques to effectively manage depression and stress. (13, 19, 20, 21)

13. Encourage the student to use words, drawings, and/or pictures to journal about past and present situations, behaviors, and feelings that are related to memories of the abuse; process the journal material.

19. Teach the student to use affirmations (e.g., "It is okay to make a mistake," "I am worthy of being loved and cared for," or "I have a right to a future") and visualizations to connect him/her to his/her positive qualities.

20. Encourage the student to check with the campus recreation center about exercise and/or intramural sports as a way to relieve stress and make safe connections with other people.

21. Review a list of relaxation techniques (e.g., massage, yoga, or meditation) and encourage the student to enroll in these or other campus wellness programs.

8. Attend a 12-Step group to learn recovery skills from addictive behaviors. (22)

22. Refer the student to the appropriate 12-Step programs on campus (e.g., AA, NA, ACOA, OA) and suggest that he/she obtain a sponsor within two weeks.

9. Utilize academic support resources to improve performance in classes. (23)

23. Assess the student's standing in current classes and refer him/her to appropriate academic resources (e.g., tutoring center, academic advisor, or meetings with professors) to ensure a successful semester.

10. Implement anger management and problem-solving skills to improve social interactions. (24, 25)

24. Teach the student techniques to manage his/her anger in healthy ways (e.g., journaling, assertive communication, hitting a heavy bag, or running).

25. Explore the student's typical responses to conflicts with authority figures (e.g., supervisors, teachers, or parents) and identify negotiation and problem-solving techniques that would provide more positive outcomes.

11. Verbalize the degree of strength of the suicidal impulse and agree to steps necessary to protect self. (26)

26. Assess the level of lethality of the student's suicidal ideation (e.g., is there a concrete plan, is there access to tools to carry out a suicide attempt such as pills, a gun, or a car, or is there a history of attempts) and require him/her to agree to a no-self-harm contract renewable every six weeks; arrange for 24-hour supervision or psychiatric hospitalization, if indicated.

12. Reduce the frequency of dissociation events. (27)

27. Teach the student to recognize specific triggers, physical cues, and particular feelings that lead to a dissociative event and

13. Implement constructive activities that will meet needs that trigger self-mutilation behavior. (28, 29)

14. Define the role that setting boundaries must play in healthy social or intimate relationships. (30, 31, 32)

encourage him/her to work at changing the pattern to stay in the present.

28. Determine the purpose served by the student's self-mutilation (e.g., to know he/she is real and alive or as punishment, tension release, or to attract attention) and assist him/her in identifying healthier ways of reaching his/her desired outcome (e.g., hit a punching bag, power walk or run, or find some company by going to a friend's room or apartment).

29. Encourage the student to participate in a campus organization that focuses on an area of personal or academic interest (e.g., the student newspaper, a retreat, or the dean's advisory council) to increase social activity that fulfills needs in a constructive manner.

30. Ask the student to read material on setting boundaries in personal relationships (e.g., *Boundaries: When You End and I Begin* by Katherine, *The Courage to Heal* by Bass and Davis, or *Boundaries and Relationships* by Whitfield); process the material read.

31. Help the student evaluate his/her ability to set appropriate limits or boundaries on relationships; explore the types of relationships he/she would like to have.

32. Assist the student in determining the boundary changes necessary to have his/her desired relationships and set specific behavioral

goals (e.g., learn to say "No," say "Hello" first, or don't allow others to assume).

15. Implement more adaptive sexual relationship practices. (33, 34, 35)

33. Refer the student to the campus health center to evaluate any ongoing physical conditions (e.g., chronic pain or STDs).

34. Encourage the student to discuss sexual concerns resulting from the abuse (e.g., flashbacks during sex, lack of sexual desire, inability to have an orgasm, fetishes, promiscuity, or dissociation during sex); process these concerns and trace their origins to childhood abuse.

35. Help the student develop a repertoire of healing responses to sexual concerns (e.g., avoid quick and impulsive involvement in sexual relations, stay in the present, have a partner who is trustworthy, stop sexual activity if necessary, or communicate honestly with his/her partner about sexual feelings).

16. Share the feelings of grief about the childhood that did not happen. (13, 36, 37)

13. Encourage the student to use words, drawings, and/or pictures to journal about past and present situations, behaviors, and feelings that are related to memories of the abuse; process the journal material.

36. Review the childhood the student had created in his/her mind and compare it to the childhood that he/she really experienced; process the feelings of grief associated with this reality.

37. Advise the student about the intensity of the grief process and

the necessity of freeing the energy used to create the illusion of a happy family and channeling it toward designing a rewarding present and future.

17. Formulate goals for the future. (38, 39, 40)

38. Ask the student to journal about his/her daydreams and hopes for the future to help him/her get in touch with possible goals.

39. Refer the student to the campus career center to begin the career exploration process.

40. Assist the student in creating a schedule that phases out therapy slowly and allows for periodic contact that will provide a sense of support and help avoid feelings of abandonment.

__. _____   __. _____
    _____   _____

__. _____   __. _____
    _____   _____

__. _____   __. _____
    _____   _____

DIAGNOSTIC SUGGESTIONS:

Axis I:	309.81	Posttraumatic Stress Disorder
	300.02	Generalized Anxiety Disorder
	300.4	Dysthymic Disorder
	309.xx	Adjustment Disorder
	296.2x	Major Depressive Disorder, Single Episode
	312.34	Intermittent Explosive Disorder
	303.90	Alcohol Dependence
	305.00	Alcohol Abuse
	304.30	Cannabis Dependence
	305.20	Cannabis Abuse
	304.20	Cocaine Dependence

305.60   Cocaine Abuse
304.89   Polysubstance Dependence
302.70   Sexual Dysfunction NOS
V71.09   No Diagnosis
799.9   Diagnosis Deferred

_____   _____

_____   _____

Axis II: 301.50   Histrionic Personality Disorder
301.83   Borderline Personality Disorder
301.82   Avoidant Personality Disorder
301.9   Personality Disorder NOS
V71.09   No Diagnosis
799.9   Diagnosis Deferred

_____   _____

_____   _____

DEPRESSION

BEHAVIORAL DEFINITIONS

1. Displays significantly sad or flat affect.
2. Experiences profound suicidal thoughts and/or engages in life-threatening actions.
3. Demonstrates increased moodiness and irritability.
4. Increasingly isolates self from roommates, significant others, class-mates, faculty, family, and/or other peers.
5. Exhibits deterioration of academic performance, athletic involvement, and/or participation in social and extracurricular activities.
6. Lacks interest in previously enjoyed activities.
7. Has a low energy level.
8. Has a significantly altered appetite.
9. Experiences sleep disturbance and lethargy.
10. Experiences intense feelings of hopelessness, worthlessness, or inappropriate guilt.

—. _____
   _____
   _____
—. _____
   _____
   _____
—. _____
   _____

LONG-TERM GOALS

1. Acknowledge the depression verbally and resolve its causes, thus leading to normalization of emotional state.
2. Reduce irritability and increase social interaction with roommates, classmates, teammates, faculty, family, and/or other friends.
3. Show a renewed typical interest in academic performance, social involvement, extracurricular activity, and eating patterns as well as occasional expressions of joy and zest for life.
4. Report normalization of eating patterns, sleeping patterns, and holding more hopeful and positive perspective about the future.
5. Seek appropriate support from roommates, significant others, peers, family, or professionals if depressed feelings or behaviors resurface.

—. _____

_____

—. _____

_____

—. _____

_____

SHORT-TERM OBJECTIVES

1. Verbalize feelings of depression and symptoms that impede functioning in classes and extracurricular activities. (1, 2, 3, 4)

THERAPEUTIC INTERVENTIONS

1. Actively build a level of trust with the student in individual sessions using consistent eye contact, active listening, unconditional positive regard, and warm acceptance of him/her to help increase his/her ability to identify and express feelings related to the depression.

2. Assist the student in identifying and clarifying depressive feelings and problems that spur depressed mood in the college setting.

3. Assess opportunities the student has taken advantage of or avoided in dealing with his/her

2. Identify unresolved issues that are contributing to depression. (5, 6)

3. Complete psychological evaluation to assess the depth of depression. (7)

4. Meet with a consulting psychiatrist or physician to facilitate evaluation of the need for antidepressant medication and/or hospitalization. (8)

5. Take psychotropic medication as prescribed and report its effect and possible side effects. (9)

6. Verbalize any history of suicide attempts or current

depression in the college environment.

4. Explore the student's history of depressed mood in the past through the present; assess whether the mood disorder is present in his/her family.

5. Explore any unresolved conflicts (e.g., family, friend, romantic, personal identity, or academic) that are contributing to the student's depression.

6. Assign the student homework of listing his/her fears associated with living away from home and family; clarify and process these unresolved fears as related to depressed feelings.

7. Conduct or arrange for psychological assessment and, after appropriate consents have been obtained, report results to the family, consulting therapist, and/or student.

8. Arrange for the student's consultation with a physician or psychiatrist to provide an examination to rule out organic causes for depression, assessment for antidepressant medication, and/or arrange for hospitalization, as appropriate.

9. Monitor and evaluate the student's psychotropic medication prescription compliance, assessing the effectiveness of the medication on his/her level of functioning and mood; consult regularly with the prescribing physician.

10. Explore the student's history and current state of suicidal urges

suicidal ideas, urges, or plans. (10, 11)

    and behavior (see Suicidal Ideation chapter in this *Planner*).

11. Arrange for the student's psychiatric hospitalization if he/she is judged to be harmful to himself/herself.

7. Contract with the therapist not to commit suicide. (10, 12)

10. Explore the student's history and current state of suicidal urges and behavior (see Suicidal Ideation chapter in this *Planner*).

12. Contract with the student, identifying what he/she will do (e.g., contact the counselor, use cognitive techniques and methods as taught in sessions, or contact a crisis line) and won't do (e.g., withdraw and avoid others or take any action that could result in any injury to himself/herself) when experiencing suicidal thoughts or impulses; provide the student with a telephone list of 24-hour emergency crisis help lines.

8. Write a description of feelings in a daily journal and track perceptions and thoughts. (13)

13. Assign the student homework of keeping a daily journal of experiences, automatic negative thoughts associated with experiences, and depressive affect that results from that distorted interpretation; process journal material to diffuse destructive thinking patterns and replace with alternate, realistic, positive thoughts, via discussion and role-play.

9. Identify distortions in thinking that lead to depressed feelings. (13, 14, 15)

13. Assign the student homework of keeping a daily journal of experiences, automatic negative thoughts associated with

experiences, and depressive affect that results from that distorted interpretation; process journal material to diffuse destructive thinking patterns and replace with alternate, realistic, positive thoughts, via discussion and role-play.

14. Teach the student the principles of cognitive therapy as a means of identifying distortions in thinking and understanding the relationship of distorted thoughts to mood alteration; help him/her recognize, express, and list his/her typical emotional responses to the cognitions that spur depressed mood.

15. Assist the student in developing awareness of cognitive messages that reinforce helplessness and hopelessness; use logic and reality testing to challenge each dysfunctional thought for accuracy, replacing it with a positive, accurate thought.

10. Complete written assignments on the cognitive aspects of depression and verbalize an understanding of how patterns of thinking affect feelings and mood. (16)

16. Assign the student written exercises (e.g., describe thoughts associated with being rejected by a classmate and the feelings produced by those thoughts) that illustrate the effect thinking has on emotions and help him/her become more aware of his/her negative thinking patterns.

11. State the connection between depression and rebellion, irritability, social withdrawal, and self-destructive behaviors. (17, 18)

17. Interpret the student's acting out behaviors (e.g., anger, irritability, substance abuse, rebellion, or isolation).

18. Assist the student in examining the connection between his/her

12. Verbalize unresolved grief issues that may be contributing to depression. (19)

13. Identify cognitive self-talk that supports social isolation. (20)

14. Replace negative and self-defeating self-talk with verbalizations of realistic and positive cognitive messages about social contact. (21, 22, 23)

15. Identify and replace irrational beliefs that spur feelings of depression. (24, 25)

previously unexpressed feelings of anger and helplessness and his/her current depression.

19. Explore the role of unresolved grief issues as contributing to the student's current depression (see the Grief/Loss chapter in this *Planner*).

20. Assist the student in identifying his/her negative, distorted self-talk that precipitates or mediates feelings of depression (e.g., "It is so lonely here, I'll never have any friends" or "Now that I'm away from home, my family will just forget about me").

21. Teach the student realistic, positive self-talk to increase his/her sense of positive perspectives or outlook (e.g., "I'm new here, but so are all the rest of the freshmen; we're all looking to make new friends" or "I should tell my family I miss them and set up times to chat on the Internet to keep in touch").

22. Assign an exercise for the student to talk positively about himself/herself into a mirror once a day; process and reinforce his/her positive statements made about himself/herself.

23. Support the student's realistic and positive verbalizations about perceptions of himself/herself, others, college life, and the world.

24. Assist the student in identifying his/her irrational beliefs that act as barriers to effective depression management (e.g., "I feel so bad, this will never change").

25. Teach the student to rationally reframe his/her irrational beliefs to remove barriers to effective depression management (e.g., "I know I feel bad today, but if I put into practice what I'm learning in sessions, I know I can work to feel better quicker"); reinforce positive, reality-based cognitive messages that can enhance self-confidence and increased adaptive reaction.

16. Implement specific behavioral responses to counteract feelings of depression. (26, 27)

26. Assist the student in developing a behavioral coping plan for each fear that is associated with depressed feelings (e.g., implementing assertiveness or social skills, initiating social contact to built a network, making contact with a spiritual support group, or utilizing tutor services on campus).

27. Assist the student in developing coping strategies (e.g., more physical exercise, less internal focus, increased social involvement, more assertiveness, greater need sharing, or more anger expression) for dealing with feelings of depression.

17. Read books or chapters as assigned on overcoming depression. (28)

28. Recommend that the student read self-help books on coping with depression (*The Feeling Good Handbook* by Burns or *What to Say When You Talk to Yourself* by Helmstetter); select chapters based on his/her needs and circumstances.

18. Increase the frequency of assertive behaviors to express needs, desires, and expectations with roommates, peers,

29. Use modeling and role playing to teach the student assertiveness skills; assign implementation of these skills to daily life

other students, and/or faculty. (29, 30)

situations and process the results.

30. Recommend that the student read books on assertiveness (e.g., *Your Perfect Right: Assertiveness and Equality in Your Life and Relationships* by Alberti and Emmons or *When I Say No, I Feel Guilty* by Smith); process concepts learned from the reading.

19. Engage in physical, recreational, and/or extracurricular activities as a depression-reduction technique. (30, 31)

30. Recommend that the student read books on assertiveness (e.g., *Your Perfect Right: Assertiveness and Equality in Your Life and Relationships* by Alberti and Emmons or *When I Say No, I Feel Guilty* by Smith); process concepts learned from the reading.

31. Explore the student's interests in recreational, athletic, and/or extracurricular activities; assign participation in at least two activities per week and process the results.

20. Apply conflict-resolution skills to unresolved interpersonal problems. (32)

32. Encourage the student to engage in routine physical exercise to stimulate depression-reducing hormones (e.g., recommend that he/she read and implement programs from *Exercising Your Way to Better Mental Health* by Leith).

21. Implement relaxation techniques during times of stress, feeling depressed, or as an aid to getting to sleep. (33)

33. Teach the student relaxation methods (e.g., progressive muscle relaxation, guided visual imagery, or deep breathing).

22. Identify a support system in the residence-hall environment that will encourage social interaction and assist with

34. Explore with the student administrative staff support (e.g., resident advisor or residence director) available to

getting past negative emotional states. (34, 35)

provide suggestions for dealing with aspects of his/her depression.

35. Reinforce the student's participation in residence-hall social activities and his/her verbalization of feelings, needs, and desires with other students.

__. _____   __. _____
    _____   _____
__. _____   __. _____
    _____   _____
__. _____   __. _____
    _____   _____

DIAGNOSTIC SUGGESTIONS:

Axis I:	300.4	Dysthymic Disorder
	309.0	Adjustment Disorder with Depressed Mood
	296.xx	Bipolar I Disorder
	296.89	Bipolar II Disorder
	301.13	Cyclothymic Disorder
	296.2x	Major Depressive Disorder, Single Episode
	296.3x	Major Depressive Disorder, Recurrent
	295.70	Schizoaffective Disorder
	V62.82	Bereavement
	_____	_____
	_____	_____
Axis II:	799.9	Diagnosis Deferred
	V71.09	No Diagnosis
	_____	_____
	_____	_____

DIVERSITY ACCEPTANCE

BEHAVIORAL DEFINITIONS

1. Reports experiencing incidents of stereotyping, prejudice, and/or discrimination during interactions on campus or in the community because of others' beliefs and feelings about his/her race, culture, ethnicity, religion, or sexual orientation.
2. Feels hostility, rage, fear, or frustration when thinking about and/or interacting with the majority culture.
3. Verbalizes stereotypic negative beliefs and intolerant attitudes toward anyone from a different cultural/sexual orientation.
4. Refuses to participate in or is openly hostile toward any environment or organization that is not specifically reflective of his/her culture/sexual orientation.
5. Academic performance and participation is mitigated by discomfort about cultural/sexual orientation and/or concerns about English fluency.
6. Will not live on campus because of cultural, religious, and/or family norms.
7. Is unable to participate in campus life beyond attending classes because of cultural, religious, and/or family norms.
8. Family determines or must approve choice of major and/or career because of cultural norms.
9. Feels overwhelmed and overburdened by family expectations based on cultural norms to assist with household responsibilities and/or financial obligations while maintaining a full academic load.

—. _____
   _____
—. _____
   _____
—. _____
   _____

LONG-TERM GOALS

1. Achieve a healthy identity by coming to terms with racial, ethnic, cultural, religious, and/or sexual orientation issues.
2. Gain a secure sense of identity by embracing membership in a minority cultural/sexual orientation while being open to other cultural/sexual orientation.
3. Feels a sense of security, confidence, acceptance, dignity, and pride that accompanies identity achievement.
4. Claim cultural/sexual orientation identity openly and publicly.
5. Be willing to negotiate/renegotiate relationships with people from the dominant or other cultural/sexual orientations.
6. Address concerns and problems of the minority culture through involvement in meaningful activities to create change.

—. _____
   _____
—. _____
   _____
—. _____
   _____

SHORT-TERM OBJECTIVES

THERAPEUTIC INTERVENTIONS

1. Identify diversity-related issues or events that are currently causing concern. (1, 2, 3, 4)

1. Explore the circumstances that cause the student to feel discriminated against and/or stereotyped.

2. Encourage the student to share any steps that he/she has taken

to gain support against the discrimination (e.g., contacted campus/community police, filed a complaint with the Dean of Students Office, or the Academic Affairs Office).

3. Suggest campus personnel that the student could contact about the discrimination.

4. Assist the student in identifying and verbalizing his/her feelings associated with the current issue(s) (e.g., rage, disgust, fear, disappointment, grief, or surprise).

2. Identify the positive and negative impact of being a member of a minority cultural/sexual orientation. (5, 6, 7, 8)

5. Ask the student what it was like to grow up in his/her particular culture or with his/her particular sexual orientation.

6. Inquire about the attitudes of the student's family toward diversity acceptance (e.g., their feelings and beliefs about accepting their own cultural/sexual orientation as well as the cultural/sexual orientations of others).

7. Trace the student's feelings about diversity acceptance to what he/she may have experienced in his/her family of origin and/or community (e.g., women should live at home until they are married; homosexuality is sinful and unnatural; or *we* can't trust *them*).

8. Invite the student to identify and discuss his/her beliefs about family with which they are currently struggling.

3. Seek academic opportunities to test beliefs and assumptions about others from a different

9. Encourage the student to register for courses that will expose him/her to his/her own cultural/

culture or sexual orientation. (9, 10, 11)

sexual orientation or to the cultural/sexual orientation of others (e.g., Muslim Theology, Latin American Literature, Sociology of Oppression, Contemporary African American Poetry, or Modern Middle East).

10. Suggest that the student register for courses taught by faculty from a minority culture.

11. Suggest that the student take courses taught by faculty who select texts and readings and conduct discussions that include a range of cultural and sexual-orientation points of view.

4. Participate in nonclassroom opportunities to test beliefs and assumptions about others from a different culture or sexual orientation. (12, 13, 14)

12. Encourage the student's connection with roommates or suitemates who share the same background to promote a sense of pride as well as individuals who can expose him/her to different cultural/sexual orientations to promote a sense of tolerance.

13. Encourage the student to contact the residence-hall administration about the availability of ongoing groups or programs within the residence halls that focus on diversity acceptance.

14. Refer the student to campus activities, multicultural affairs, office for international students, and/or religious ministry to connect with organizations and programming for students from minority cultural/sexual orientations (e.g., Black student organizations, Latino student organizations, Hillel, or Gay, Lesbian, Bisexual, Transgender and Questioning youth groups).

5. Participate in service learning, community service, or volunteer projects within the community that will challenge beliefs and assumptions about the similarities and differences among and within people from various cultural/sexual orientations. (15, 16)

6. Increase contact with those who will be empathetic about experiences of cultural/sexual orientation intolerance. (17, 18, 19)

7. Clarify academic major and/or career interests that comply with cultural and family expectations. (20, 21, 22, 23)

15. Suggest that the student register for a course that has a service-learning component that requires his/her active involvement in his/her own cultural/sexual orientation or in the cultural/sexual orientation of another.

16. Link the student to religious ministry immersion trips or community service programs that will open the doors of a different cultural/sexual orientation.

17. Refer the student to faculty and/or staff that are actively involved in social justice and/or diversity acceptance efforts.

18. Refer the student to bilingual or international support services, if language is a concern.

19. Support the student's connection with older students who have had similar experiences as members of a minority culture and have developed adaptive coping skills.

20. Discuss the student's concerns about selecting a major/career and determine whether family involvement is an issue.

21. Refer the student to the career center for career testing and/or research of occupations that would be satisfying for the student as well as comply with family dictates.

22. Role-play a discussion between the student and family members to help the student present his/her findings and the careers options that are of interest to him/her.

23. Endorse the student's participation in career-related organizations that work specifically with students from minority cultures (e.g., Hispanic Alliance for Career Enhancement for Latino students or INROADS for African American students) to acquire experience and career mentors.

8. Acknowledge the importance of family support while recognizing that certain beliefs and assumptions will no longer be shared with them. (24, 25)

24. Support the student cognitively and emotionally as he/she begins to identify and adopt beliefs and lifestyle behaviors that differ from his/her family of origin.

25. Help the student find opportunities to maintain family connections while being congruent with his/her own emerging values and beliefs.

9. Take leadership roles in student organizations to improve interactions with peers from both the minority and dominant cultural/sexual orientations. (26, 27, 28)

26. Encourage the student to run for office or to chair an event sponsored by his/her own minority group's organization to learn to communicate effectively with peers of similar background.

27. Suggest that the student move his/her student organization toward cosponsoring events with student groups of different backgrounds to learn to effectively communicate and negotiate with people unlike him/her.

28. Ask the student to consider a leadership role in a student organization that does not focus on cultural/sexual

10. Participate in community organizations that promote equality for people from all cultures and sexual orientations. (29, 30, 31)

orientation and has a mixed membership.

29. Recommend that the student discuss his/her interest in participating in wider social justice arenas with his/her mentors and seek their recommendations.

30. Assist the student in researching the missions and projects of community organizations and selecting at least one in which to participate.

31. Provide ongoing support for the student's campus and community work that promotes interaction with people from a variety of cultures and sexual orientations.

__. _____   __. _____
    _____   _____

__. _____   __. _____
    _____   _____

__. _____   __. _____
    _____   _____

DIAGNOSTIC SUGGESTIONS:

Axis I:	V62.4	Acculturation Problem
	308.3	Acute Stress Disorder
	V71.01	Adult Antisocial Behavior
	312.30	Impulse-Control Disorder
	V71.09	No Diagnosis
	799.9	Diagnosis Deferred
	_____	_____
	_____	_____

Axis II: 301.7   Antisocial Personality Disorder
301.9   Personality Disorder NOS
301.20   Schizoid Personality Disorder
V71.09   No Diagnosis
799.9   Diagnosis Deferred

_____   _____

_____   _____

EATING DISORDERS

BEHAVIORAL DEFINITIONS

1. Chronically and rapidly consumes large quantities of high carbohydrate foods.
2. Frequently self-induces vomiting after eating because of fear of weight gain.
3. Frequent abuses laxatives because of fear of weight gain.
4. Has had an extreme weight loss (and amenorrhea in females) and refuses to maintain a minimal healthy weight.
5. Ingests a very limited amount of food and frequently engages in secret, self-induced vomiting; inappropriate use of laxatives; and/or excessively strenuous exercise.
6. Is persistently preoccupied with body image due to a grossly inaccurate assessment of self as overweight.
7. Has a predominating irrational fear of becoming overweight.
8. Presents with an escalating fluid and electrolyte imbalance resulting from poor dietary habits.

—. _____
_____
—. _____
_____
—. _____
_____

LONG-TERM GOALS

1. Establish healthy eating pattern, appropriate body weight, balanced fluid intake, appropriate electrolyte levels, and/or realistic perception of body size.
2. Terminate patterns of binge eating and vomiting with a return to ingestion of appropriate amount of nutritious foods to maintain healthy weight.
3. Expand understanding of the cognitive and emotional issues underlying the eating disorder.
4. Develop alternative coping strategies (e.g., feeling identification or assertiveness) to deal with underlying emotional issues, thereby making the eating disorder unnecessary.
5. Heighten awareness of the interconnectedness of low self-esteem, control concerns, and cultural pressures with dieting, binge eating, and purging.
6. Restructure the definition of the self so that it does not focus on weight, size, and shape as the primary or sole criteria for self-acceptance.
7. Recognize distorted thoughts and dysfunctional beliefs and values that contribute to eating-disorder development.
8. Follow through consistently with lifestyle changes to address emotional and psychological improvements as well as healthy eating habits while at school and at home.

—. _____
_____
_____
—. _____
_____
_____
—. _____
_____

SHORT-TERM OBJECTIVES

THERAPEUTIC INTERVENTIONS

1. Honestly describe eating pattern frequency, amounts, and types of food consumed or hoarded. (1, 2, 3, 4)

1. Actively build a level of trust with the student using consistent eye contact, active listening, unconditional positive regard, and warm acceptance to increase his/ her ability to identify and express feelings related to

concerns about body image and eating.

2. Explore the student's current eating pattern as well as perception of body image.

3. Assist the student in identifying and clarifying specific feelings and concerns that spur inappropriate dietary actions in the college setting (e.g., underlying fears related to the eating disorder), noting any habit of self-induced vomiting to control caloric intake, regular use of laxatives to reduce body weight, and/or frequent use a vigorous exercise to control weight gain.

4. Explore the student's history of managing weight, stress, and/or family and social relationships in high school through the present.

2. Identify how maladaptive eating behaviors are related to an attempt to manage academic and social stresses of college life. (5, 6)

5. Explore the relationship between the student's stress related to campus life (e.g., academic pressures, social adjustment, or emancipation struggles) and his/her eating disorder.

6. Teach the student about the importance of learning to manage stress appropriately, seek support, and use therapy.

3. Identify the relationship between the fear of failure in academic or social performance, the drive for perfectionism, and the eating disorder. (7, 8)

7. Discuss the student's fear of failure and the role of perfectionism in the search for control and avoidance of failure.

8. Confront the student's irrational perfectionism in body image expectations and assist in his/her reasonable acceptance of the flawed body.

4. Identify and replace irrational thoughts and expectations about body size. (9, 10)

9. Help the student clarify the reasons for his/her eating behaviors, as they are related to body image and eating habits.

10. Confront the student's unrealistic assessment his/her body image and assign exercises (e.g., positive self-talk in the mirror or shopping for clothes that flatter the appearance) that reinforce the healthy, realistic body appraisal.

5. Acknowledge to family members the feelings of ambivalence related to control and separation. (11, 12, 13, 14)

11. Involve the family in conjoint student therapy sessions to increase familial support and understanding and develop more adaptive parenting skills.

12. Facilitate family therapy sessions with the student that focus on owning feelings, clarifying messages, identifying control conflicts, and developing age-appropriate boundaries.

13. Teach the student's parents or his/her significant other how to successfully detach from taking responsibility for his/her eating behavior without becoming hostile or indifferent.

14. Support and encourage the student in identifying fears related to separation aimed at making a declaration of independence from his/her family; encourage the parents to support the student's burgeoning independence.

6. Participate in family sessions to address issues concerning dietary and lifestyle habits, emotional needs, and

13. Teach the student's parents or his/her significant other how to successfully detach from taking responsibility for his/her eating

behavioral expectations for school and home. (13, 15)

7. Verbalize the connection between suppressed emotional expression, difficulty with interpersonal issues, and unhealthy food usage. (16)

8. Cooperate with a medical evaluation and physical examination. (17, 18)

9. Take psychotropic medication as ordered and report effectiveness and side effects. (18, 19)

10. Cooperate with admission to an inpatient treatment program if a

behavior without becoming hostile or indifferent.

15. Recommend that the student's parents, significant other, or friends read *Surviving an Eating Disorder* (Siegel, Brisman, and Weinshel); process the concepts in family therapy sessions.

16. Teach the student about the connection between suppressed emotions, interpersonal conflict, and dysfunctional eating behavior.

17. Refer the student to a physician or to the campus clinic for a thorough medical evaluation; refer the student back to his/her physician on regular intervals if fluids and electrolytes need monitoring because of poor nutritional habits.

18. Refer the student to a psychiatrist to evaluate the severity of the student's eating disorder and determine the need for psychopharmacological intervention and/or hospitalization.

18. Refer the student to a psychiatrist to evaluate the severity of the student's eating disorder and determine the need for psychopharmacological intervention and/or hospitalization.

19. Monitor the student for psychotropic medication prescription compliance and side effects; confer with the prescribing physician at regular intervals.

20. Refer the student for hospitalization if his/her weight loss

fragile medical condition necessitates such treatment. (20)

11. Comply with a dental exam to check for concerns secondary to vomiting. (21)

12. Submit to a daily weighing by an appropriate person. (22)

13. Eat at regular intervals (three meals a day), consuming at least the minimum calories daily (established by physician, nutritionist, and/or counselor) necessary to progressively gain weight. (23, 24)

14. State a basis for positive identity that is not based on weight and appearance but character, traits, relationships, and intrinsic value. (25)

15. Understand and verbalize the connection between excessively restrictive, unhealthy

becomes severe and physical health is jeopardized.

21. Refer the student to a dentist for an examination if purging/vomiting is reported or suspected.

22. Weigh the student daily and log his/her weight at a consistent time; assign this task to a roommate, campus clinic staff, or other objective person. Monitor the student's weight and give him/her weekly realistic feedback about body fitness.

23. Refer the student to a dietitian for education about healthy eating and nutritional concerns; process the student's meeting with the nutritionist on concrete plans for meal planning and caloric consumption.

24. Establish healthy weight goals for the student using the Body Mass Index (BMI = Pounds of body weight × 700/height in inches/height in inches; normal range is 19 to 25 and below 18 is medically critical), the Metropolitan Height and Weight Tables, or some other recognized standard.

25. Teach and reinforce the student's acceptance of himself/herself and others as human and subject to shortcomings and imperfection; if appropriate, use his/her spiritual belief system to strengthen this concept.

26. Encourage the student to read books on binging eating (e.g., *Overcoming Binge Eating* by

dieting and binge episodes. (26)

16. Identify negative self-talk and substitute with positive, healthy, and rational self-talk associated with healthy eating and engage in normal food intake. (27, 28, 29)

17. Verbalize acceptance of sexual impulses and the desire for intimacy. (30, 31)

Fairburn) to increase awareness of the components of eating disorders.

27. Assist the student in identifying his/her negative, distorted self-talk that precipitates or mediates the desire to engage in eating-disordered behavior(s) (e.g., "I am so fat, no one will ever want to go out with me," "Everyone else here is so skinny, I'll never be that thin," or "It's okay if I pig out this weekend, it's been so stressful this week, I deserve it!").

28. Teach the student realistic, positive self-talk to increase his/her sense of control over the desire to engage in eating-disordered behavior(s) (e.g., "I am five pounds over my ideal body weight for my size, with a rational plan, I should be able to loose it in four to six weeks," "While everyone else looks great, I have some good friendships starting," or "This was a tough week, but if I spend time with my friends, practice my relaxation techniques, and listen to some music I can avoid my typical pig outs").

29. Train the student to establish realistic cognitive messages about food intake and body size; reinforce his/her use of more realistic, positive messages to himself/herself about food intake and body size.

30. Discuss the student's fear of losing control of sexual impulses and how the fear

relates to keeping himself/
herself unattractively thin or fat.

31. Reinforce the acceptance of
sexual impulses and desire for
intimacy as normal in the
student.

18. Verbalize the acceptance of
full responsibility for choices
about eating behavior and
accept personal responsibility
for adequate nutrition as
evidenced by progressive
weight gain or maintenance of
adequate weight without the
supervision of others. (32, 33)

32. Monitor the student's vomiting
frequency, food hoarding,
exercise levels, laxative usage,
and weight gain on an ongoing
basis, expecting a weight gain of
two pounds per week.

33. Reinforce the student's weight
gain and acceptance of personal
responsibility for normal food
intake.

19. Keep a journal of feelings and
emotions to improve awareness of negative distortions of
self-image and body image,
which leads to eating disorder
behaviors. (27, 28, 34)

27. Assist the student in identifying
his/her negative, distorted self-
talk that precipitates or mediates
the desire to engage in eating-
disordered behavior(s) (e.g., "I
am so fat, no one will ever want
to go out with me," "Everyone
else here is so skinny, I'll never
be that thin," or "It's okay if I
pig out this weekend, it's been
so stressful this week, I deserve
it!").

28. Teach the student realistic,
positive self-talk to increase
his/her sense of control over
the desire to engage in eating-
disordered behavior(s) (e.g., "I
am five pounds over my ideal
body weight for my size, with
a rational plan, I should be able
to loose it in four to six weeks,"
"While everyone else looks
great, I have some good
friendships starting," or "This
was a tough week, but if I
spend time with my friends,

practice my relaxation techniques, and listen to some music I can avoid my typical pig outs").

34. Assign the student homework of keeping a journal of daily thoughts and feelings associated with eating behaviors; process journal information.

20. Implement assertive behaviors to allow an adaptive and healthy self-expression of needs and emotions. (35, 36)

35. Train the student in assertiveness or refer to an assertiveness training class.

36. Reinforce assertive behaviors in each session and reports of the student's successful assertiveness between sessions.

21. Implement behavioral and cognitive coping strategies to deal with stressors that act to perpetuate the eating disorder. (37)

37. Assist the student in developing a behavioral coping plan (e.g., learning assertiveness or social skills, initiating social contact, or making contact with a spiritual support group) for occasions when he/she is tempted to binge, purge, abuse laxatives, overexercise, and/or fast.

22. Identify distorted self-talk beliefs associated with eating normal amounts of food and replace irrational beliefs that block effective dietary habits. (38, 39)

38. Assist the student in identifying his/her irrational beliefs that spur the desire to engage in eating-disordered behavior(s) (e.g., "I know all the girls use laxatives, so what if I do too?").

39. Teach the student to rationally reframe his/her irrational beliefs to remove barriers from dealing with the desire to engage in eating-disordered behavior(s) (e.g., "Even if others abuse laxatives to try to be thin, I know that doesn't work very well; and it really causes more problems that just aren't worth it").

23. Attend an eating-disorder support group and participate actively. (40)

24. Identify a support system in the residence-hall environment that will encourage and assist in dealing with the eating disorder. (41, 42)

25. Display a stable medical condition as measured by physical examination, blood work, and appropriate weight and maintain balanced fluids and electrolytes (established by the physician, nutritionist, and/or counselor) as well as resumption of reproductive functions (if a female with amenorrhea). (24, 32, 33, 43)

40. Refer the student to an appropriate community resource self-help group (e.g., Anorexia Nervosa Anonymous); encourage attendance and process the experience in session.

41. Explore the peer resources (e.g., planned group activities, socials, study groups) available to the student in mediating or offering suggestions to deal with the desire to engage in eating-disordered behavior(s).

42. Explore administrative staff support (e.g., resident advisor, residence director) available to the student; provide him/her suggestions to deal with the desire to engage in eating-disordered behavior(s).

24. Establish healthy weight goals for the student using the Body Mass Index (BMI = Pounds of body weight × 700/height in inches/height in inches; normal range is 19 to 25 and below 18 is medically critical), the Metropolitan Height and Weight Tables, or some other recognized standard.

32. Monitor the student's vomiting frequency, food hoarding, exercise levels, laxative usage, and weight gain on an ongoing basis, expecting a weight gain of two pounds per week.

33. Reinforce the student's weight gain and acceptance of personal responsibility for normal food intake.

43. Maintain contact with the
    student's physician to ensure
    that he/she is medically stable
    and returning to normal weight
    and electrolyte balance.

__. _____   __. _____
    _____   _____

__. _____   __. _____
    _____   _____

__. _____   __. _____
    _____   _____

DIAGNOSTIC SUGGESTIONS:

Axis I: 307.1   Anorexia Nervosa
                 307.51   Bulimia Nervosa
                 307.50   Eating Disorder NOS
                 300.4   Dysthymic Disorder

                 _____   _____

                 _____   _____

Axis II: 301.6   Dependent Personality Disorder
                 799.9   Diagnosis Deferred
                 V71.09   No Diagnosis

                 _____   _____

                 _____   _____

FAMILY RELATIONSHIP CONFLICTS

BEHAVIORAL DEFINITIONS

1. Thinking about family or visits home is accompanied by negative feelings, such as anxiety, depression, anger, guilt, shame, sadness, fear, or frustration.
2. Returns home as often as possible to fix problems and/or to keep things from falling apart.
3. While at school is often called on to mediate family conflicts and solve family problems.
4. Avoids going home, even during holidays and school breaks.
5. Is unable to effectively manage interpersonal conflicts within the family or with peers.
6. Worries excessively about the opinions and approval of family members, teachers, roommates, and/or friends.
7. Goes to great lengths to meet family member's needs, often sacrificing personal needs and/or responsibilities.
8. Uses alcohol or other substances to escape from stress.
9. Fears destined to be just like his/her mother and/or father.

—. _____
   _____
—. _____
   _____
—. _____
   _____

LONG-TERM GOALS

1. Understand the impact of family patterns of interaction on the formation of identity, self-esteem, and self-efficacy.
2. Understand the impact of family patterns of interaction on access to a range of feelings, rational thought processes, and personal power.
3. Learn to construct, value, and maintain physical, intellectual, emotional, social, sexual, financial, and time boundaries in all relationships.
4. Maintain rational beliefs about personal worth, abilities, and responsibilities.
5. Communicate needs effectively and resolve conflicts within the family and with peers.
6. Institute respectful and independent patterns of interaction with family.

—. _____
   _____
—. _____
   _____
—. _____
   _____

SHORT-TERM OBJECTIVES	THERAPEUTIC INTERVENTIONS
1. Identify current interpersonal relationship concerns with family members. (1, 2, 3)	1. Invite the student to explain the specific family issue that is of immediate concern.
	2. Ask the student to describe, as fully as possible, the nature of his/her interactions with family members since he/she has been in college.
	3. Explore the student's history of family interactions as well as his/her specific feelings about the immediate problem (e.g., mad, sad, glad, or none).
2. Explore patterns of interaction among family members. (4, 5)	4. Assist the student in creating a genogram to identify critical information about family members (e.g., age, occupation,

or health) as well as the type and quality of connections among them (e.g., enmeshed, cut off, or triangulated), using concepts from Lerner's *Dance of Intimacy*.

5. Explore the impact of family patterns of conditional love, addictions, illness, impulsivity/compulsivity, abuse, violence, or abandonment on the student's current self-image and relationships with peers.

3. List family rules/norms and their impact on current feelings and behavior. (6, 7)

6. Provide poster paper and have the student use the genogram information to list the overt/covert family rules that he/she lived by when at home as well as the rules that are still in force while he/she is at school.

7. Help the student focus on his/her current relationships and note whether the family rules that continue to direct his/her beliefs and behaviors are enhancing his/her life or making it more difficult.

4. Reject and/or rewrite family rules to make them more appropriate for current life roles and goals. (8, 9, 10)

8. Ask the student to identify and reframe the family rules that are irrational and to write his/her new rules on another sheet of poster paper (e.g., "The only acceptable grade is an A." versus "I will work to learn something rather than stride for the grade"; "Relationships always end badly, so what's the point?" versus "I am willing to alter my behaviors that contribute to creating unhealthy relationships"; "I must always respond to the needs of others." versus "It is important to keep

my own needs as well as the needs of others in mind when deciding on a course of action").

9. Suggest that the student identify the revised rule(s) that can be applied to the current family issue and discuss the feeling, thinking, and behavioral changes that would be necessary to implement these new rules.

10. For homework, encourage the student to hang the new rules poster paper in his/her bedroom, using it for affirmation and to direct his/her choices feelings, thoughts, and behaviors toward family and others.

5. Implement assertive communication in interaction with family members. (11, 12, 13)

11. Help the student define aggressive, passive, and assertive communication styles and review the effect of his/her preferred style (e.g., Aggressive = Ensuring that my needs are met without concern or respect for the needs of another; Passive = Ensuring another's needs are met without concern or respect for my own needs; Assertive = Ensuring that my needs as well as another's are considered and respected when determining a course of action); discuss how assertiveness can be applied to his/her family conflicts.

12. Teach the student the DESC approach (adapted from *Asserting Yourself* by Bower and Bower) to assertive communication (e.g., **De**scribe the concern in behavioral terms: "I paid our phone bill two weeks ago. At the time, I showed you the bill and asked for your share of

the money but have yet to receive it." Express the emotion: "I am annoyed that you haven't said anything about the money you owe me and frustrated because I was short of cash this week." Specify the behavior change you are seeking: "I would like you to pay your share of a bill at the same time that I make the payment. If you don't have the money on that particular day, I would like you to tell me when you will be able to pay me back." State the Consequences: "If you will let me know your financial situation at the time I am paying bills, I am sure that we can work out a plan that will suit both of us. This way, I won't be upset with you or have to struggle to meet my expenses").

13. Ask the student to create a DESC script and role-play this conversation, using the current family problem, to ensure that he/she feels as comfortable as possible in his/her new assertive role.

6. Explore and utilize a range of nurturing techniques to reduce family stress and enhance self-esteem. (14, 15, 16)

14. Suggest that the student read *Growing Up Again* (Clarke and Dawson) to understand the importance of family nurture in human development; process the role nurture played in his/her family.

15. Help the student explore the possibilities of nurturing activities on campus (e.g., yoga class or similar programs offered at the campus recreation center, guided meditation or other programs offered at the wellness

center, or liturgies offered through the campus ministry center) and nurturing techniques that he/she can use any time (e.g., music, reading, walking, or connecting with nature) to counteract the feelings of rejection from family members.

16. Encourage the student to include play and leisure time in his/her life (e.g., biking, rollerblading, intramural teams, picnics, or massage) as a distraction from the stress of family issues and a broadening of life activities; invite him/her to select one activity from each category and incorporate them into his/her life each week.

7. Terminate the use of substances as a way to manage feelings, relax, and/or cope with family stress. (17, 18)

17. Ask the student to describe his/her use of alcohol or other substances to have a good time; assess whether substance abuse is being used as an escape from family stress (see Chemical Dependence/Abuse chapter in this *Planner*).

18. If abuse/addiction is a concern, encourage the student to attend 12-Step meetings on campus and monitor his/her efforts to control use and/or abstain.

8. Establish appropriate interpersonal boundaries with family members. (19, 20, 21)

19. Assist the student in understanding the concepts of connection, individuation and differentiation as they relate to his/her family relationships (see *Growing Up Again* by Clarke and Dawson, *The Dance of Intimacy* by Lerner, and *Family Evaluation: An Approach Based on Bowen Theory* by Kerr and Bowen).

20. Conduct an exploration of the boundary issues within the student's family using the genogram and discus how these issues affect his/her ability to thrive in college.

21. Encourage the student to create a plan of action to establish boundaries with family members: Reduce the number and length of phone calls from home by (a) letting family members know that the amount of time spent on the phone diminishes the time needed for school, (b) asking them to use e-mail instead of the phone, (c) suggesting that you will call them at least once a week when you have more time to talk, or (d) screen phone calls; ask the student to share this plan with family member(s).

9. Maintain boundaries with family members in spite of their change-back messages. (22, 23, 24, 25)

22. Prepare the student for change-back messages from the family (e.g., helping him/her understand that phone calls from family are likely to increase or stop completely rather than decrease as requested) and that maintaining the new boundary during this time of pressure is imperative to achieving the goal.

23. Help the student recognize the feelings that will accompany a change-back message (e.g., anxiety about angering or losing the other; guilt about not responding immediately to another's needs; or fear that something bad will happen because you refused to respond); teach the student that these

feelings cannot be avoided, but they will pass.

24. Suggest that the student keep a feelings journal to vent his/her feelings about the process of setting boundaries with family members and to help prevent him/her from acquiescing to family members' inappropriate demands.

25. Support the student through the process of establishing and maintaining boundaries by discussing his/her progress weekly.

10. Report improved relationships with family. (26, 27)

26. Use modeling and role-play to teach the student the use of assertive communication to maintain appropriate boundaries of independence with family members.

27. Meet weekly with the student for a full semester, sustaining him/her through the processes required to improve relationships with family and others.

__. _____   __. _____

_____   _____

__. _____   __. _____

_____   _____

__. _____   __. _____

_____   _____

DIAGNOSTIC SUGGESTIONS:

Axis I:

313.82	Identity Problem
309.24	Adjustment Disorder with Anxiety
296.2x	Major Depressive Disorder, Single Episode
305.20	Cannabis Abuse
305.00	Alcohol Abuse
V62.89	Phase of Life Problem
V71.09	No Diagnosis
799.9	Diagnosis Deferred

_____ _____

_____ _____

Axis II:

301.6	Dependent Personality Disorder
301.9	Personality Disorder NOS
V71.09	No Diagnosis
799.9	Diagnosis Deferred

_____ _____

_____ _____

FINANCIAL STRESS

BEHAVIORAL DEFINITIONS

1. Lacks funds to pay for tuition, room, and board, jeopardizing academic enrollment.
2. Expenditures regularly outweigh income or budget.
3. Parents' ability to contribute toward college expenses is significantly diminished because of a change in family circumstances (e.g., divorce, unemployment of a parent, or illness of a family member).
4. Is unable to work the number of hours necessary to meet expenses without sacrificing academic success.
5. Cannot cover college expenses with income from financial aid package.
6. Is unable or unwilling to find a part-time job that blends with the academic schedule and responsibilities.
7. Lacks information on and/or experience with the basics of personal finance (e.g., creating a budget, paying monthly bills, or balancing a checkbook).
8. Withdraws cash through ATMs without tracking amounts or balances.
9. Puts small purchases (e.g., gas, groceries, or fast food) on credit cards because cash in unavailable.
10. Is unable to make more than the minimum payment on credit cards, resulting in continuous high balances and interest payments.
11. Borrows money from one source to pay off another (e.g., using credit card to pay for rent).
12. Compromises credit rating because of late payment or nonpayment of bills.

—. _____
   _____
—. _____
   _____
—. _____
   _____

LONG-TERM GOALS

1. Research information to improve financial aid package.
2. Create a realistic annual budget identifying all school and living expenses.
3. Clarify family contributions and personal contributions toward college costs.
4. Develop strategies to accurately track income and expenditures.
5. Develop strategies to ensure that decisions about purchases are made within the context of a realistic budget.
6. Obtain employment that offers flexibility around academic schedules and provides a wage that will help pay for college expenses and contribute to debt reduction.
7. Eliminate dependency on credit cards.

—. _____
   _____
—. _____
   _____
—. _____
   _____

SHORT-TERM OBJECTIVES

1. Identify the particular financial issues that are currently a source of stress. (1, 2)

THERAPEUTIC INTERVENTIONS

1. Ask the student to list every concern that he/she is currently facing about his/her financial situation.

2. Explore how each of the student's financial concerns developed over time.

2. Discuss family attitudes toward money management and financial independence. (3, 4)

3. Investigate the role that money played in the student's family of origin (e.g., power, control, independence/dependence, or status).

4. Assist the student in becoming aware of his/her beliefs and feelings about money and how they are related to his/her experiences within the family (e.g., money will always be there for me, we always spend more than we have, creditors have always chased us, or money buys respect).

3. Commit to making the changes in attitude and lifestyle necessary to successfully resolve financial concerns. (5, 6, 7)

5. Assist the student in reframing his/her beliefs about money that have had a detrimental effect on his/her interest in and ability to effectively manage money.

6. Assign the student homework of writing a list of behavioral changes necessary to improve his/her financial picture (e.g., creating a budget, balancing the checkbook, cutting up credit cards, or getting a job).

7. Obtain the student's commitment to implementing the money management changes that will immediately improve the financial picture and reduce stress.

4. Gather information necessary to create a realistic picture of income and expenditures. (8, 9, 10, 11)

8. Suggest that the student read books on budgeting (e.g., *Dollars and Sense for College Students* by Braitman) to gather ideas for improving money management and financial planning.

9. Assign the student homework of performing an expense analysis

by tracking every purchase or expenditure (no matter how small) for one full week.

5. Identify and apply for available financial aid for college expenses. (12, 13, 14, 15)

10. Ask the student to list all income and expenditures for one month, using the Sample Budget worksheets in *Dollars and Sense for College Students* (Braitman) and the results of the expense analysis.

11. Review the student's monthly budget and explore areas for possible change.

12. Refer the student to a campus financial aid advisor to review his/her aid package in light of changes in the student's ability to contribute.

13. Refer the student to a list of books and web sites that identify scholarships and grants (e.g., the college's financial aid web site, www.fastweb.com [free scholarship search], www.finaid.org/scholarships/unusual.phtml, *How to Find Out About Financial Aid and Funding 2003–2005* by Schlachter, and *Peterson's Scholarships, Grants, and Prizes 2004*).

14. After the student has researched grants and scholarships, suggest he/she identify at least 10 to contact for further information, tracking specific application requirements and deadlines for each.

15. Guide and encourage the student through the grant and scholarship application processes (e.g., check timelines, or critique essays).

6. Search for and procure part-time employment. (16, 17, 18)

16. Ask the student to list his/her criteria for part-time employment (e.g., ideal number of hours per week and schedule, salary range required, or job duties); examine this list, helping him/her refine job criteria and identifying possible types of employment and/or employers.

17. Refer the student to the campus career center to investigate employment opportunities both on and off campus and to meet with a career counselor who could mentor him/her through the job-search process.

18. Monitor the progress of the student's job search and of his/her movement toward academic as well as financial goals once the job is obtained.

7. Reduce the role that credit plays in current and future financial plans. (19, 20, 21)

19. Ask the student to identify purchases made on credit, using the expense analysis, and determine whether they were essential and how payment could have been made in some other way.

20. Explore the specific problems that have been created by the student's use of credit (e.g., paying high interest rates on high balances, owing more than income allows, buying impulsively, receiving calls from creditors, or jeopardizing school enrollment).

21. Assist the student in listing and prioritizing necessary changes in his/her use of credit (e.g., cut up high-interest/high-balance cards

and close accounts, ask lenders for lower interest rates, pay as much above the minimum payment as possible, or contact consumer credit service to negotiate with lenders).

8. Implement cost-cutting options to reduce monthly expenses. (22, 23)

22. Review the student's bills and brainstorm changes to reduce them (e.g., maintain a 68 to 70 degree thermostat setting, turn off all electronic devices when not in use, shop at discount or warehouse grocery stores, use generic brands, or change to a cheaper phone company).

23. Help the student identify all nice-to-have-but-not-essential expenses and encourage him/her to consider cancellation or a major change (e.g., cable, cell phone, Internet access, magazine subscriptions, commuting from home versus living on campus, selling a car, or taking public transportation versus keeping a car on campus).

9. Meet with family to discuss financial status and concerns and to define their role in the larger financial picture. (24, 25, 26, 27)

24. Ask the student to write a list of topics that should be covered in a family meeting about his/her finances (e.g., current budget, actions already taken to increase income and decrease expenses, financial contributions that the family currently provides, or financial problems still faced by the student).

25. Encourage the student to enlist family members' help in the problem-solving process by asking for their ideas and opinions as well as providing possible solutions for consideration.

26. Role-play the family meeting about finances with the student to ensure that he/she is able to communicate directly and respectfully with family members.

27. Process the student's family meeting about finances, helping him/her make budget revisions based on the meeting outcome.

10. Adjust the budget based on new income and expense projections. (28, 29)

28. Encourage the student to make revisions to his/her budget and financial plan based on new income (e.g., part-time job, parent assistance, scholarships, and grants) and cost cutting.

29. Meet with the student biweekly for the remainder of the academic year to provide direction and support for his/her efforts to effectively manage his/her finances.

11. Create a five-year plan that identifies major life goals and a long-range budget that will support these goals. (30, 31, 32)

30. Ask the student to read *Life After Graduation: Financial Advice and Money Saving Tips* (Arndt and Ricchini); process long-range financial plans.

31. Brainstorm financial issues with the student to be considered when developing a five-year plan (e.g., school loan repayment, insurance, day-to-day living expenses, savings options, or investment possibilities).

32. Suggest that the student meet with a financial planner to solidify a plan for major life goals (e.g., travel, study abroad, or graduate school) and begin taking appropriate actions.

—. _____   —. _____
    _____   _____
—. _____   —. _____
    _____   _____
—. _____   —. _____
    _____   _____

DIAGNOSTIC SUGGESTIONS:

Axis I:

308.3	Acute Stress Disorder
300.02	Generalized Anxiety Disorder
300.00	Anxiety Disorder NOS
309.xx	Adjustment Disorder
V62.2	Occupational Problem
V62.89	Phase of Life Problem
V71.09	No Diagnosis
799.9	Diagnosis Deferred

_____   _____

_____   _____

Axis II:

301.9	Personality Disorder NOS
V71.09	No Diagnosis
799.9	Diagnosis Deferred

_____   _____

_____   _____

GRADUATION ANXIETY

BEHAVIORAL DEFINITIONS

1. Thoughts of graduation evoke conflicting emotions including excitement, anxiety, happiness, fear, numbness, sadness, love, loneliness, or relief.
2. Verbalizes persistent somatic complaints (e.g., headache, stomachache, or sleeping problems) associated with stress.
3. Forgets to fulfill college's requirements for graduation (e.g., meeting with an academic advisor to ensure all coursework is complete, applying for graduation, ordering a cap and gown, or paying outstanding bills and fees).
4. Experiences anxiety that severely blocks or compromises the ability to complete a final piece of required academic work (e.g., senior thesis, senior recital, research project, or portfolio).
5. Avoids graduation by changing major during the final year of school, ensuring another semester or two of new courses.
6. Procrastinates on finalizing postgraduation living arrangements (e.g., pack up dorm room or apartment, discuss living arrangements with appropriate family members, or secure a place to live).
7. Avoids taking the steps necessary to successfully search for a job or graduate program (e.g., resume is not prepared, occupational or organizational research has not been compiled, or applications are not submitted).
8. Wavers about or does not include family members in graduation ceremonies or postgraduation plans.
9. Refuses to attend graduation ceremonies or celebrations or to say good-bye to anyone of significance at school.
10. Doubts the ability to be independent and is overwhelmed by the personal responsibility associated with being a self-sufficient adult.

—. _____
_____

—. _____
_____

—. _____
_____

LONG-TERM GOALS

1. Recognize and effectively manage the intellectual and emotional tasks associated with college graduation.
2. Understand and accept that separation and independence are processes that do not occur in a single moment; they are composed of many events, interactions, feelings, and personal insights.
3. Accept the reality of imminent change and consciously own responsibility for the future.
4. Learn to say good-bye and bring positive closure to relationships.
5. Develop a vision of the future and take the risks necessary to make it happen.

—. _____
_____

—. _____
_____

—. _____
_____

SHORT-TERM OBJECTIVES

1. Describe the behavioral and emotional responses to the process of completing college and becoming independent. (1, 2, 3, 4)

THERAPEUTIC INTERVENTIONS

1. Assist the student in identifying and thoroughly exploring specific events and/or problems that have hampered his/her adjustment to graduating and moving on.

2. Assign the student a journal to track his/her thoughts and

concerns about leaving college, feelings associated with these issues, and the contexts that trigger these thoughts and emotions.

3. Help the student clarify the reasons for her/his maladaptive behaviors throughout this final year of college, using journal entries and the graduation story.

4. Encourage the student to explore his/her feelings associated with finishing school, paying particular attention to which feelings were freely expressed, suppressed, considered inappropriate, or denied in some way.

2. Identify core issues highlighted by the graduation transition. (5)

5. Distill the student's information about graduation-related thoughts and feelings, identifying key life issues, core emotions, and contextual patterns.

3. Verbalize an understanding of the feelings associated with the graduation experience. (6, 7, 8)

6. Provide the student with a transitional-stage model to help normalize and process his/her feelings and experiences (see *Learning to Leave: Problems of Graduating* by Margolis) by identifying the four stages of graduation as (a) identifying and completing tasks, (b) anticipating change, (c) participating in the ceremony, and (d) moving on.

7. Introduce the student to the paradox of graduation, that is, an event that signals many endings (losses) as well as many beginnings (opportunities); process this paradox as it applies to the student's losses and opportunities.

8. Suggest that the student read *Procrastination* (Burka and Yuen) to better understand her/his difficulty with completing tasks.

4. Implement a plan of action to complete academic requirements for graduation. (9, 10, 11, 12)

9. Ask the student to list every academic responsibility that must be completed by graduation day (e.g., portfolio, research papers, internship hours, meetings with academic advisor, or submission of all documents necessary for graduation).

10. Assist the student in developing objectives and deadlines for each academic responsibility that must be completed before graduation.

11. As homework, ask the student to use easel paper to chart his/her progress on academic tasks on a time line that can be posted in a prominent location in his/her living space.

12. Require the student to provide weekly updates on her/his progress toward meeting these academic responsibilities.

5. Cooperate with a medical evaluation for somatic concerns. (13)

13. Refer the student to the campus health center to determine whether there is a physiological basis for somatic complaints.

6. Utilize stress-management techniques to cope more effectively with graduation transitions. (14, 15, 16)

14. Teach the student anxiety-reduction techniques (e.g., deep breathing, positive imagery, deep muscle relaxation, and positive self-talk) to help him/her cope with stress precipitated by graduation (see *The Relaxation and Stress Reduction Workbook* by Davis, Eshelman, and McKay or *Ten Days to Self-Esteem* by Burns).

7. Replace distorted, anxiety-producing thoughts with realistic thoughts that elicit confidence. (17, 18)

8. Seek assistance with career and job-search plans. (19, 20)

15. Ask the student to create a list of stress-management techniques that he/she has successfully used in the past (e.g., increased exercise; consistent sleeping pattern; attention to nutrition; visualization; meditation; massage; or spending time with positive, supportive friends) and incorporate several of these into his/her daily routine.

16. Refer the student to and encourage him/her to participate in a stress-management group.

17. Assist the student in identifying his/her distorted negative thoughts (e.g., "I'm not ready to take on the responsibilities of a new career position," "I'll never land a job with all the competition out there," or "I'm going to fail on my final assignments and not be eligible to graduate") that precipitate graduation anxiety.

18. Assist the student in replacing his/her distorted thoughts with realistic, positive thoughts (e.g., "I'm well prepared to enter a career position"; "I will present myself to potential employers with confidence and enthusiasm"; and "I have proven myself as a capable student, so I can handle these final academic hurdles just fine") that promote feelings of confidence, calm, and excitement when approaching graduation (see *What to Say When You Talk to Yourself* by Helmstetter).

19. Refer the student to the campus career center for assistance with

immediate and long-term career decisions and the job search.

20. Review the student's resume, asking him/her to elaborate on the objective and experience sections to emphasize and encourage ownership of particular strengths and skills.

9. Finalize postgraduation housing plans. (21, 22, 23)

21. Ask the student to list in order of preference his/her housing options on easel paper (e.g., stay in current apartment, find a new roommate, or move back home).

22. For homework, encourage the student to select her/his two best housing options and develop a plan of action for each.

23. Touch base at each session about the student's progress toward finalizing a housing plan and make course corrections as necessary.

10. Share postgraduation plans and feelings with family members. (24, 25)

24. Suggest that the student share his/her academic challenges and housing and job concerns as well as general feelings about graduation with an adult family member.

25. Role-play a conversation between the student and a family member that encourages the student to communicate his/her thoughts and feelings directly, honestly, and respectfully.

11. Discuss the calendar of graduation events with family members. (26, 27, 28)

26. Review the graduation events hosted by the university and encourage the student to partici- pate in at least one event.

27. Suggest that the student contact her/his family, inviting them to

the graduation event(s) in which he/she will participate.

28. Consider the kind of family celebration that the student would enjoy and support the student's efforts to communicate these desires to his/her family.

12. Identify and utilize personal strengths to successfully negotiate the graduation process. (29, 30, 31)

29. Invite the student to discuss other successful transitions he/she has made, identifying the skills and talents he/she utilized to meet the challenges posed by change.

30. Help the student identify his/her skills and strength patterns after having listened to several transition stories.

31. Encourage the student to identify current situations that would be improved or corrected by applying his/her skills and talents to the graduation process.

13. Verbalize resolution of emotional struggles related to graduation issues. (18, 32, 33)

18. Assist the student in replacing his/her distorted thoughts with realistic, positive thoughts (e.g., "I'm well prepared to enter a career position"; "I will present myself to potential employers with confidence and enthusiasm"; and "I have proven myself as a capable student, so I can handle these final academic hurdles just fine") that promote feelings of confidence, calm, and excitement when approaching graduation (see *What to Say When You Talk to Yourself* by Helmstetter).

32. Process the questions that are of greatest concern to the student (e.g., "Will I make it?" "Who will be there for me?" "Will my

past accomplishments count for anything now?" or "What does success look like to me?") to reduce fear and anxiety.

33. Normalize the student's conflicts over his/her contradictory feelings about graduation as well as his/her struggle with graduation transitions.

14. Bring closure to college relationships that will be altered by or discontinued because of graduation. (34, 35, 36, 37)

34. Suggest that the student list every relationship that will be affected by graduation (e.g., friends, roommates, favorite professors, advisors, or parents) and determine the best way to say good-bye (e.g., e-mail, thank-you note, personal visit, or dinner).

35. Role-play a saying good-bye conversation with the student.

36. Encourage the student to visit favorite campus locations to say farewell and move on.

37. Suggest that the student create a scrapbook or photo album of favorite college people and places as a tribute and farewell.

15. Replace recollections of the past with visions and goals for the future. (38, 39, 40, 41)

38. Invite the student to write a personal mission statement to bring her/his vision for the future into focus.

39. Assist the student in developing goal statements based on his/her mission, assigning deadlines for accomplishment; challenge him/her to take personal responsibility for realizing these goals.

40. Assist the student in identifying individuals who could mentor his/her vision and mission;

encourage him/her to contact these people and ask for their support.

41. Use weekly sessions to monitor the student's progress through every aspect of the graduation transition process.

__. _____   __. _____
    _____   _____
__. _____   __. _____
    _____   _____
__. _____   __. _____
    _____   _____

DIAGNOSTIC SUGGESTIONS:

Axis I:

309.24	Adjustment Disorder with Anxiety
309.0	Adjustment Disorder with Depressed Mood
309.3	Adjustment Disorder with Disturbance of Conduct
308.3	Acute Stress Disorder
300.02	Generalized Anxiety Disorder
313.82	Identity Problem
V62.3	Academic Problem
V62.89	Phase of Life Problem
V71.09	No Diagnosis

_____ _____

_____ _____

Axis II:

301.82	Avoidant Personality Disorder
301.83	Borderline Personality Disorder
301.9	Personality Disorder NOS
V71.09	No Diagnosis

_____ _____

_____ _____

GRIEF/LOSS

BEHAVIORAL DEFINITIONS

1. Thoughts dominated by loss coupled with poor concentration in class and other settings, tearful spells, and confusion about what to do.
2. Has recently experienced serial losses in life (i.e., deaths, divorce of parents, or moves) that have led to a depressed mood and discouragement.
3. Exhibits a strong emotional response when personal losses are discussed.
4. Experiences a lack of appetite, weight loss, and/or insomnia as well as other signs of depression since the loss.
5. Feels guilt that not enough was done to prevent the loss or has an unreasonable belief of having contributed to the loss.
6. Avoids talking at any emotional depth about the loss.
7. The geographic move to live on campus has resulted in a loss of a positive support network.

—. _____
   _____
—. _____
   _____
—. _____
   _____

LONG-TERM GOALS

1. Begin a healthy grieving process around the loss.
2. Develop an awareness of how the avoidance of grieving has negatively affected his/her life and begin the healing process.
3. Complete the process of letting go of the lost significant other or secure situation.

4. Resolve the loss and begin initiating new contacts with others on campus and elsewhere.

—. _____

_____

—. _____

_____

—. _____

_____

SHORT-TERM OBJECTIVES

THERAPEUTIC INTERVENTIONS

1. Identify the loss(es) experienced and give detailed history of those that are triggering problems/symptoms. (1, 2)

2. Begin verbalizing feelings associated with the loss. (3, 4)

3. Identify the emotional and behavioral impact of the loss. (5, 6)

1. Explore the facts surrounding the student's history of loss.

2. Ask the student to elaborate in an autobiography on the circumstances of the loss(es) in his/her life.

3. Actively build a level of trust with the student in individual sessions using consistent eye contact, active listening, unconditional positive regard, and warm acceptance to help increase his/her ability to identify and express thoughts and feelings.

4. Assist the student in identifying and clarifying his/her specific feelings and problems that relate to his/her loss as he/she tries to cope in the college setting.

5. Explore the student's process of dealing with his/her feelings of grief and loss through the present time; explore the impact of the grief on his/her social, academic, and emotional adjustment.

4. Verbalize an increased understanding of the steps in the
   grieving process. (7, 8)

5. Read material on the topic of
   grief to better understand the
   experience and increase a
   sense of hope. (9, 10, 11)

6. Attend a grief support group.
   (12)

7. Identify how the avoidance of
   dealing with the loss has had a
   negative impact. (13)

6. Assess opportunities the student
   has taken advantage of or avoided
   to cope with feelings of grief and
   loss in the college environment.

7. Educate the student on the
   stages of the grieving process
   and answer any questions
   related to this process as he/she
   has experienced it.

8. Ask the student to talk to several
   people about losses in their
   lives, especially how they felt
   and coped; process his/her
   interview experiences, summarizing what he/she learned
   about the grief process.

9. Request that the student read
   books dealing with grief and
   loss (e.g., *Good Grief* by
   Westberg, *How Can It Be All
   Right When Everything Is All
   Wrong* by Smedes, or *When Bad
   Things Happen to Good People*
   by Kushner).

10. Request that the student's par-
    ents read *The Bereaved Parent*
    by Schiff; process the key
    themes gained from the reading.

11. Ask the student to watch films
    (e.g., *Terms of Endearment,
    Dad*, or *Ordinary People*) that
    focus on loss and grieving;
    discuss how the characters cope
    with loss and express their grief.

12. Refer the student to a grief/loss
    support group and process the
    experience of attending.

13. Ask the student to list ways that
    avoidance of grieving has
    negatively impacted his/her life
    and the college experience.

8. Identify how the abuse of alcohol/substances has aided in the avoidance of feelings associated with the loss. (14, 15)

9. Verbalize and resolve feelings of anger or guilt focused on self or lost loved one that blocks the grieving process. (16, 17, 18)

10. Identify the causes of feelings of regret associated with actions toward or relationship with the deceased. (19)

11. Express thoughts and feelings about the deceased that went unexpressed while the deceased was alive. (20, 21)

14. Assess the role of substance abuse as an escape from the pain of grief.

15. Arrange for chemical dependence treatment so grief issues can be faced while the student is clean and sober (see Chemical Dependence/Abuse chapter in this *Planner*).

16. Explore the student's feelings of anger or guilt that surround the loss, helping him/her understand the sources for such feelings.

17. Encourage the student to forgive himself/herself and/or the deceased to resolve feelings of guilt or anger; recommend books on the topic of forgiveness (e.g., *Forgive and Forget: Healing the Hurts We Don't Deserve* by Smedes or *The Art of Forgiving* by Smedes).

18. Assign the student homework of writing a letter to the deceased describing fond memories, painful and regretful memories, last meaningful contact, and how he/she currently feels; read the letter in the session and process the content.

19. Assign the student homework of making a list of all the regrets he/she has concerning the loss and process the list in session.

20. Conduct an empty-chair exercise with the student where he/she focuses on expressing to the lost loved one (imagined to be in the empty chair) what he/she never said.

21. Direct the student to visit the grave of the loved one, talk to

12. Identify the positive character-
    istics of the deceased loved
    one, the positive aspects of the
    relationship with deceased
    loved one, and how these
    things can be remembered
    appropriately. (22, 23, 24, 25)

13. Implement behavioral coping
    strategies to work through
    grief and loss. (26, 27)

    the deceased, and ventilate
    feelings.

22. Ask the student to list the most
    positive aspects of the memories
    about the relationship with the
    lost loved one.

23. Ask the student to bring pictures
    or mementos connected with the
    loss to session and discuss their
    meaning.

24. Assist the student in developing
    rituals (e.g., place memoriam in
    newspaper on anniversary of
    death, volunteer time to a
    favorite cause of the deceased
    loved one, eat a meal at the
    deceased's favorite restaurant, or
    place flowers at a church
    service) that will celebrate the
    memorable aspects of the
    deceased loved one's life.

25. Request that the student research
    activities, interests, commit-
    ments, loves, and passions of the
    lost loved one and select an
    activity (community service
    connected) to do in his/her honor.

26. Assist the student in developing
    a behavioral coping plan for
    each problematic aspect of the
    grieving process (e.g., initiating
    social contact to build a suppor-
    tive network, making contact
    with a spiritual support group, or
    utilizing tutor services on
    campus to get back on track
    with academic requirements).

27. Use role-play and modeling to
    teach the student assertive dialog
    that respectfully identifies issues
    or needs in behavioral terms,
    recognizes both individuals'

needs and rights, and offers possible solutions that are mutually beneficial; encourage him/her to implement assertiveness to increase socialization and to verbalize needs and desires.

14. Identify and replace distorted self-talk that precipitates or perpetuates disturbing emotions while working through grief and loss. (28, 29, 30)

28. Assist the student in identifying his/her negative, distorted self-talk that precipitates or mediates feelings of sadness, isolation, anxiety, or defensiveness/distrust (e.g., "I will never be as happy as I was before this happened to me"; "No one can understand what it is like to go through this pain"; "I can never finish college now that this has happened"; or "Everyone acts like they want to help me, but they really don't care").

29. Teach the student realistic, positive self-talk to increase his/her sense of peace and resilience in dealing with the loss (e.g., "I am a reasonable and intelligent person; therefore, I can learn to get beyond this"; "I do have people who do care about me"; or "I can still accomplish what I have set out to do in spite of this setback").

30. Use a Rational Emotive Therapy approach to gently confront the student's irrational, distorted statements of responsibility for the loss and compare them to reality-based facts.

15. Identify and replace irrational beliefs that block effective resolution of feelings associated with grief and loss. (31, 32)

31. Assist the student in identifying his/her irrational beliefs that act as barriers to effective coping (e.g., "Everyone thinks I'm making this a bigger deal than it really is," "My life is ruined

forever now," or "I cannot ever put this behind me").

32. Teach the student to rationally reframe his/her irrational beliefs to remove barriers to coping effectively (e.g., "Most people also have experienced this and have been just fine," "I have to believe that I can deal with this effectively over time with the help and support that I have" or "Learning new ways to deal with the loss make sense and are within my abilities to use and practice").

16. Decrease by _____% the time spent daily focusing on the loss. (33, 34, 35)

33. Suggest that the student set aside a specific time-limited period each day to focus on mourning his/her loss; after each day's time is up, he/she resumes regular activities and puts off grieving thoughts until the next scheduled time.

34. Direct the student to engage in at least one social interaction activity per day and record his/her feelings about these experiences in a journal.

35. Assist the student to identify how he/she depended on the significant other, expressing and resolving the accompanying feelings of abandonment and being left alone; encourage him/her to reach out to build a broad social support network.

17. Identify a support system in the college environment that will encourage and assist with working through grief and loss. (36, 37)

36. Explore peer resources (e.g., supportive roommate, close friends, church group, or grief support group) available to the student in helping to cope with and manage difficult emotions.

18. Attend and participate in family therapy sessions focused on each member sharing his/her grief experience. (38)

19. Implement acts of spiritual faith as a source of comfort and hope. (39, 40)

37. Explore administrative staff support (e.g., resident advisor or residence director) available to provide the student with a listening ear and make suggestions when times get difficult.

38. Conduct a session with the family and student allowing each member to talk about his/her experience related to the loss.

39. Encourage the student to rely on his/her spiritual faith practices, activities (e.g., prayer, meditation, worship, or music), and fellowship as sources of support.

40. Refer the student to a pastor, priest, or rabbi who can provide spiritual counseling related to the loss.

—. _____

—. _____

—. _____

—. _____

—. _____

—. _____

DIAGNOSTIC SUGGESTIONS:

Axis I: 309.0   Adjustment Disorder with Depressed Mood
309.3   Adjustment Disorder with Disturbance of
Conduct
296.2x   Major Depressive Disorder, Single Episode
296.3x   Major Depressive Disorder, Recurrent
V62.82   Bereavement
300.4   Dysthymic Disorder

_____   _____

_____   _____

Axis II: 799.9   Diagnosis Deferred
V71.09   No Diagnosis

_____   _____

_____   _____

HOMESICKNESS/EMANCIPATION ISSUES

BEHAVIORAL DEFINITIONS

1. Constantly focuses thoughts on home (i.e., parents, siblings, extended family, friends, or pets).
2. Feels anxious, confused, sad, and/or angry when thinking of home.
3. Makes contact with home almost daily.
4. Almost never makes contact with home and family.
5. Refuses to interact with others, severely limiting the development of new relationships.
6. Overinvolves self in new relationships, severely constricting personal time to reflect, grieve, or adjust to emancipation.
7. Bases decisions on pleasing or punishing family or others rather than taking personal needs, hopes, values, skills, and goals into account.
8. Lacks self-knowledge and/or is uncomfortable with the sense of self.
9. Fears others' disapproval of experimentation with new roles and lifestyles.
10. Lacks the ability to identify and develop an effective support system during times of transition.

__. _____

_____

__. _____

_____

__. _____

_____

LONG-TERM GOALS

1. Effectively manage the intellectual and emotional tasks of leaving home and family.
2. Understand and accept both loss and adventure as inherent parts of the process of emancipating from the family.
3. Become aware of and participate in opportunities that are available in a collegiate environment to explore roles and experiment with lifestyles.
4. Scan the environment for opportunities to connect with individuals and groups that both challenge and support the emerging self-concept.
5. Embrace identity, using the sense of self to inform decision making.

—. _____

_____

—. _____

_____

—. _____

_____

SHORT-TERM OBJECTIVES

THERAPEUTIC INTERVENTIONS

1. Discuss the difficulties experienced in achieving a satisfying transition to college. (1, 2)

1. Assist the student in identifying and clarifying specific feelings and problems that hamper her/his adjustment to school.

2. Assess opportunities the student has taken advantage of or avoided to become connected to the college environment.

2. Tell the complete story of leaving for college, identifying emotional and behavioral responses to leaving home. (3, 4, 5)

3. Explore the student's process of leaving home, beginning with applying to college through the present.

4. Help the student clarify the reasons for his/her behaviors during the process of leaving home, beginning with applying to college through the present.

3. Identify the responses of family to this and previous experiences with leaving home. (6, 7)

4. Clarify core concerns about leaving home. (8, 9, 10, 11)

5. Create a safe physical space at school to reduce anxiety

5. Encourage the student to focus on the feelings associated with leaving home, specifically those that were permitted, considered inappropriate, or denied in some way.

6. Help the student identify behaviors demonstrated and feelings expressed by others during the leaving-home process.

7. Assist the student in recognizing his/her family patterns of leaving with particular attention to dysfunctional responses (e.g., anger, denial, anxiety, avoidance, and refusal to accept leaving as permanent).

8. Assign the student a journal to track her/his thoughts and concerns about leaving home, feelings associated with these issues, and the context in which these thoughts and feelings emerge.

9. Review the student's homework on thoughts and feelings about leaving home, identifying key issues, predominant feelings, and contextual patterns.

10. Make connections between the student's core concerns about leaving home and his/her family's responses to clarify his/her current feelings and behaviors.

11. Introduce the student to the concept of the inherent paradox of leaving home, which is that leaving home is both a loss and an adventure.

12. Encourage the student to settle into his/her dorm room to create

caused by the transition.
(12, 13, 14, 15)

a familiar, personal space (e.g.,
unpack completely, display
photos of important people/
events, or stock fridge and room
with comfort food).

13. Determine whether the student
brought transitional objects from
home and whether he/she is
using them to reduce anxiety
(e.g., pictures, stuffed animals,
sports equipment, a scrapbook, a
favorite book, or a small piece
of furniture).

14. Explore the student's sleep
patterns and suggest options if
his/her typical pattern appears
disturbed by the new environment (e.g., refrain from taking
naps during the day, get up at
the same time each morning,
curb intake of caffeine and
nicotine, and establish and
maintain a bedtime routine).

15. Assist the student in creating a
study space based on his/her
needs and what he/she was used
to at home (e.g., complete quiet
versus background noise, library
versus dorm room, access to a
computer, or individual versus
group preferences).

6. Maintain, within reasonable
boundaries, meaningful contact
with family and friends from
home. (16, 17, 18, 19)

16. Encourage the student to use e-
mail or cards to connect with
family and friends from home;
when the content of conversation has the potential to be
emotionally charged or dependency enhancing, suggest that the
student refrain from instant-
messaging to curb anxiety/
depression and maintain healthy
boundaries.

17. Assist the student in setting realistic limits on the number of family contacts per week and/or amount of time spent in contact with the family.

18. Encourage the student to initiate some form of connection (e.g., letter, card, e-mail, phone call, or visit) at least once a week if contact with home has been cut off.

19. Help the student sift through the type and amount of information that would be useful to share with family and friends as a means of keeping connected with home.

7. Identify and utilize personal strengths to act independently. (20, 21, 22)

20. Explore the degree of the student's emotional dependence on one or both parents and the family dynamics that have nurtured this dependence (e.g., dominating or critical parents or symbiotic parent connections).

21. Assist the student in identifying his/her strengths (e.g., intelligence, judgment, or social skills) that can serve as a basis for making the break from dependence on parents and siblings.

22. Assist the student in developing a plan of action to become more independent with the campus culture that capitalizes on his/her strengths.

8. Implement behavioral and cognitive coping strategies to overcome emancipation fears. (23, 24, 25)

23. Assign the student homework of listing his/her fears associated with living away from home and family; clarify and process these fears.

24. Assist the student in developing a behavioral coping plan for each fear that is associated with the emancipation process (e.g., learning assertiveness or social skills, initiating social contact to build a network, making contact with a spiritual support group, or utilizing tutor services on campus).

25. Assist the student in identifying his/her negative and distorted self-talk that nurtures the fear and anxiety associated with emancipation; replace the distorted self-talk with positive, realistic messages that promote confidence and independence.

9. Increase the frequency of social contact with peers to meet the need for affiliation and increase a sense of belonging. (26, 27, 28)

26. Contract with the student to sit with other students for meals in one of the campus dining halls versus eating meals alone.

27. Assist the student in identifying other students that offer possibilities for social connection (e.g., roommates, suitemates, resident assistant, classmates, or student clubs or organizations).

28. Model and role-play initial meetings and conversations to help the student feel at ease with the process of meeting and connecting with new people.

10. Gather information related to groups, programs, classes, and special events that match personal interests and values. (29, 30)

29. Direct the student to vehicles for information about campus happenings (e.g., student newspaper, bulletin boards, university or student organization web sites, campus radio station, e-mail notices about

meetings and special events, or student mailbox).

30. Encourage the student to check with the residence-hall staff, academic advisors, student affairs staff, and faculty for information about university and/or community activities and events.

11. Increase involvement in clubs, organizations, athletics, spiritual activities, or employment. (31, 32, 33, 34)

31. Suggest that the student attend campus organization fairs, introductory meetings of clubs, rush, or other informational sessions that might fit his/her interests and values.

32. Support the student's inquiries into on-campus employment, intramural sports, spiritual activities, fitness classes, volunteer options, campus government, ministry retreats, and/or special events.

33. Help the student sort through information on clubs, organizations, academic disciplines, community programs, and work opportunities to select a few key activities in which to fully participate.

34. Encourage the student to evaluate his/her level of participation and continuing interest at several points during the semester to decide on continued commitment as well as alterations in the number of organizations or activities in which he/she is involved.

12. Seek experienced individuals willing to serve as role models and mentors. (35, 36)

35. Promote the student's ongoing contact with a faculty advisor, favorite faculty and/or staff member, or student officer of a club or organization of interest.

36. Encourage the student to investigate opportunities for volunteer work, leadership training, research under the guidance of a faculty member, and/or participation in a career-mentor program.

13. Make decisions based on personal values and identity. (37, 38)

37. Teach the student the decision-making model inspired by James March (see *A Primer on Decision Making: How Decisions Happen* by March) that includes three main questions: (a) What kind of situation is this? (b) Who am I? and (c) How should a person like me act in a situation like this one?

38. Encourage the student to read *A Primer on Decision Making: How Decisions Happen* (March) and discuss applying the process to a current decision the student must make.

14. Journal about how the emancipation process is helping to define own identity. (39, 40)

39. Assign the student readings that bring to life the losses and adventures of leaving home (e.g., *The Alchemist* by Coelho or *Callings: Finding and Following an Authentic Life* by Levoy); ask him/her to journal about applying key ideas to his/her life and then process key ideas in session.

40. Ask the student to keep a journal that charts movement toward defining self (e.g., list needs, skills, talents, valued relationships, interests, values, hopes, dreams, or fears) and review entries for feedback and suggestions.

__. _____   __. _____
     _____   _____
__. _____   __. _____
     _____   _____
__. _____   __. _____
     _____   _____

DIAGNOSTIC SUGGESTIONS:

Axis I: 309.0   Adjustment Disorder with Depressed Mood
               309.3   Adjustment Disorder with Disturbance of
                         Conduct
               309.24   Adjustment Disorder with Anxiety
               309.28   Adjustment Disorder with Mixed Anxiety and
                         Depressed Mood
               300.23   Social Phobia
               300.02   Generalized Anxiety Disorder
               300.4   Dysthymic Disorder

               _____   _____
               _____   _____

Axis II: 301.20   Schizoid Personality Disorder
               301.6   Dependent Personality Disorder

               _____   _____
               _____   _____

INTIMACY/COMMITMENT ISSUES

BEHAVIORAL DEFINITIONS

1. Fearful of making a marriage commitment as a viable relationship option.
2. Equates a sexual relationship with genuine and meaningful intimacy.
3. Becomes involved in a sexual relationship without taking time to get to know the other person.
4. Ignores school, family, and friendship commitments to spend time with a partner.
5. Is unable to achieve a balance between feeling close to someone and maintaining a separate identity.
6. Is habitually attracted to unattainable partners.
7. Refuses to express feelings of love for fear of appearing weak or being rejected.
8. Terminates a relationship as soon as the other person becomes emotionally involved.
9. Discontinues all other relationships or is not truthful with his/her partner about maintaining interactions with other people.
10. Consistently over- or underfunctions in a relationship.

—. _____
   _____
—. _____
   _____
—. _____
   _____

LONG-TERM GOALS

1. Understand the components of a healthy intimate relationship.
2. Identify and begin the reparation of developmental delays related to the ability to achieve strong, positive interpersonal relationships.
3. Select a partner who can offer the possibility of a healthy relationship.
4. Maintain appropriate interpersonal boundaries.
5. Continue progress toward academic and career goals as well as building a relationship with a partner.
6. Preserve other relationships while developing a relationship with a partner.

—. _____

_____

—. _____

_____

—. _____

_____

SHORT-TERM OBJECTIVES	THERAPEUTIC INTERVENTIONS
1. Identify current relationship problems and patte~	1. Ask the student to describe the facts and dynamics of his/her current relationship.
	. Explore the issues that make the student's relationship difficult or threaten its continuation.
	Assist the student in recognizing problem patterns in his/her relationships and verbalize his/her feelings about them.
	sess whether the same tionship problem patterns aced in the student's ionships with family bers.
	te the student about the of family-of-origin issues evelopment of rigid

153

boundaries, unable to maintain boundaries, inability to express feelings, or fear of asking for needs and wants) on his/her ability to sustain healthy, intimate relationships.

6. Ask the student to read *The Dance of Intimacy* (Lerner); process issues about intimacy conflicts and the role of family-of-origin experiences.

7. Connect the student's current beliefs about his/her functioning in relationships to his/her family-of-origin issues (e.g., emotionally absent parent; divorced parents; parent controlling through abuse; overprotective or negligent parent; parents' addictions).

3. Identify and replace distorted and dysfunctional self-talk with positive and realistic messages about relationships. (8, 9, 10)

8. Reframe the student's dysfunctional, negative thoughts and beliefs about loving and being loveable (e.g., "Everyone cheats on his/her partner" versus "Many people are trustworthy and faithful," "I'm spoiled and no one will ever want to meet my needs" versus "I can develop a partnership based on trust and mutuality," "Why would anyone want me?" versus "I'm a good person and someone will be very lucky to have me as a partner").

9. Encourage the student to review relationships with other partners, recognizing the historical, negative messages that were given to him/her are now affecting the current relationship (e.g., "You'll never find anyone who will love you as much as I do"; "You need someone to take care

of you"; "You won't make it without me"; or "You're too [dumb, fat, shy, poor] for anyone else to care about").

10. Assist the student in developing cognitive and behavioral responses that significantly reduce the negative expectations and low self-image brought into the current relationship (e.g., create and prominently post affirmations in his/her living space that combat negative messages; make a CD of positive, encouraging music that will boost his/her mood in moments when he/she is questioning his/her worth; or develop a list of factual responses that counter the negative, inaccurate messages and keep it handy at all times).

4. Identify the characteristics of a strong, positive relationship with a partner. (11, 12, 13)

11. Ask the student to read material on building intimate relationships (e.g., *If the Buddha Dated* by Kasl and *Men, Women and Relationships* by Gray); discuss concepts from the material read that are related to characteristics of healthy relationships.

12. Encourage the student to synthesize information from various sources and write his/her personal list of characteristics that he/she believes are necessary to develop and maintain a relationship with a significant other.

13. Using the student's relationship characteristics list, assist him/her in evaluating his/her current relationship and suggest that he/she share perceived strengths

5. Verbalize a distinction among intimacy, passion, and commitment. (14)

6. Express thoughts and feelings directly, effectively, and respectfully. (15, 16)

7. Implement attentive, active listening skills. (17, 18, 19)

and weaknesses with his/her partner.

14. Using Sternberg's model of love, help the student understand the differences among intimacy, passion, and commitment (Intimacy = Closeness, affection, connectedness; Passion = Sex drive, physical closeness, romance; Decision/ commitment = Decision to or recognition of love followed by the commitment to maintain love); ask him/her to complete Sternberg's Triangular Love Scale (see *The Triangle of Love* by Sternberg) and process the results.

15. Teach the student to use I statements that are direct, honest, respectful and avoid blaming, shaming or accusing others; ask him/her to use this technique as much as possible during counseling sessions when discussing his/her feelings.

16. Use a feelings chart to help the student learn a range of words to describe, clarify, and share his/her feelings appropriately.

17. Teach the student the elements of effective nonverbal communication (e.g., maintain eye contact, remove external distractions like the television or cell phone, or nod or give some nonverbal cue to encourage the speaker to continue); use modeling and role-play to apply these skills.

18. Provide the student with information on reflective listening and offer him/her opportunities to learn this skill through the use of role-playing and modeling.

19. Suggest that the student read the chapter on Habit #5: "Seek first to understand and then to be understood" in *The Seven Habits of Highly Effective People* (Covey); discuss how this principal can be applied to his/her relationships.

8. Attempt to resolve conflict issues with inconsistent partner while implementing respectful guidelines for discussions. (20, 21, 22, 23)

20. Help the student determine his/her ground rules for settling disagreements (e.g., remember you are both in this together or avoid personal attacks and bringing up past issues and concentrate on present concerns).

21. Suggest to the student that the time and place for a discussion be negotiated to avoid trying to solve problems when either partner is too tired, angry, drunk, or sick to fully participate.

22. Provide the student with fair fighting guidelines (e.g., be specific about his/her concerns; take on one issue at a time; ask for a change that is realistic and reasonable; recognize that he/she must hear out the partner and also be willing to change; and understand that resolving some issues requires time, patience, and commitment).

23. Remind the student to end attempts to resolve conflicts with some expression of

appreciation for the partner's efforts and recognition of the importance of the relationship.

9. Implement activities that are focused on increasing intimacy and connection with the partner. (24, 25, 26)

24. Assist the student in understanding the concepts of connection, individuation, and differentiation as they relate to his/her current relationship (see *Family Evaluation: An Approach Based on Bowen Theory* by Kerr and Bowen, *The Dance of Intimacy* by Lerner, and *If the Buddha Dated* by Kasl).

25. Suggest that the student and his/her partner read *The Couple's Comfort Book* (Louden) and select activities that would enhance their level of intimacy (connection) and their ability to establish boundaries in the context of their relationship.

26. Recommend that the student and his/her partner share their answers to questions from *If. . .* (McFarland and Saywell) and/or *The Hard Questions* (Piver) to generate discussion on important topics, recognize their similarities, and understand and accept their differences.

10. Improve and maintain academic performance while devoting time to a relationship. (27, 28, 29, 30)

27. Recommend that the student review the syllabi from all current courses to identify areas where he/she has fallen behind.

28. Encourage the student to meet with professors to negotiate deadlines or extra assignments to catch up and/or improve academic standing.

29. Advise the student to employ time-management techniques to

ensure that adequate time is available for academic work and employment.

30. Ask the student to provide a weekly update on his/her academic and job performance.

11. Increase socialization with a broad range of friends and through a variety of interesting activities. (31, 32, 33)

31. Encourage the student to identify relationships that have diminished or ended because of his/her involvement with a partner.

32. Help the student determine ways to repair former relationships and to meet new people to broaden and maintain his/her social network.

33. Recommend that the student become actively involved in areas of interest by renewing his/her membership in related student organizations or seeking student/community groups that are focused on his/her interests.

12. Identify and resolve feelings of fear about making a commitment to intimacy with a partner. (34, 35, 36)

34. Explore the student's fears of an intimate relationship and the related fear of making a commitment.

35. Process the student's fear of rejection or abandonment as related to intimate relationships.

36. Encourage the student to use the share-check method of taking small steps to *share* intimate feelings of vulnerability with a partner and then *check* whether the trust was rewarded by respect, kindness, and reciprocity.

—. _____   —. _____
    _____   _____
—. _____   —. _____
    _____   _____
—. _____   —. _____
    _____   _____

DIAGNOSTIC SUGGESTIONS:

Axis I: 300.2   Generalized Anxiety Disorder
                300.00   Anxiety Disorder NOS
                313.83   Identity Problem
                309.24   Adjustment Disorder with Anxiety
                301.13   Cyclothymic Disorder
                302.70   Sexual Dysfunction NOS
                V62.89   Phase of Life Problem
                V71.09   No Diagnosis
                799.9   Diagnosis Deferred

                _____   _____
                _____   _____

Axis II: 301.9   Personality Disorder NOS
                301.83   Borderline Personality Disorder
                V71.09   No Diagnosis
                799.9   Diagnosis Deferred

                _____   _____
                _____   _____

LEARNING/PHYSICAL DISABILITIES

BEHAVIORAL DEFINITIONS

1. Lower academic achievement is the suspected result of perceptual disabilities, brain injury or dysfunction, dyslexia, or developmental aphasia.
2. The learning disability substantially interferes with academic performance or with basic daily living skills requiring reading, math, and/or written language.
3. Has a physical disorder that limits mobility and movement and distorts posture (e.g., cerebral palsy, muscular dystrophy, spina bifida, osteogenesis imperfecta [brittle bone disease], amputation [limb deficiency], and spinal cord injuries).
4. Feels frustrated, anxious, angry, and/or inadequate when thinking about academic requirements.
5. Avoids new or challenging academic situations based on a belief that no amount of effort will ensure a positive outcome.
6. Fears feeling the embarrassment, criticism, and/or disappointment that have historically accompanied attempts to achieve academically and/or interpersonally.
7. Exhibits inappropriate, awkward, and/or defensive behaviors in interpersonal situations that keep others at a distance.
8. Often does not complete assignments for classes or never starts them and attends class erratically.
9. Is unable/unwilling to advocate for needed accommodations with professors or college administrators.
10. Physical discomfort/pain often inhibits academic performance and social interactions.
11. Uses substances to blunt difficult feelings and experiences.

—. _____
    _____
—. _____
    _____
—. _____
    _____

LONG-TERM GOALS

1. Improve academic functioning substantially in deficit areas over the long term.
2. Maintain the maximum mobility and access within the school environment.
3. Adopt a sense of self that recognizes the disability as a significant but single component of a much larger life.
4. Understand the facts about and be proactive in the management of the disability.
5. Learn to advocate for accommodations necessary to achieve academically and socially.
6. Develop realistic academic expectations and personal habits that will nurture their achievement.
7. Develop a career plan.

—. _____
    _____
—. _____
    _____
—. _____
    _____

SHORT-TERM OBJECTIVES

1. Clarify the facts about the disability. (1, 2, 3)

THERAPEUTIC INTERVENTIONS

1. Assess the student's factual understanding of his/her disability.

2. Request permission to review the documentation of his/her

disability and discuss this information with the student to ensure a clear and shared view of factual information about the academic and social impact of his/her disability.

3. If no documentation is available, refer the student to the campus coordinator of services for students with disabilities to obtain referrals to campus or community resources that can assess and document the student's disability.

2. Share feelings and fears regarding the effect of the disability on academic performance and social acceptance. (4, 5, 6)

4. Ask the student to list all academic and social problems that he/she believes are a direct result of his/her disability.

5. Help the student identify and reframe any cognitive distortions that he/she may have about the disability (e.g., "A disability is a neurological or physical condition" versus "A disability is a character defect, moral shortcoming, or fatal flaw"; "Intelligent people can also be learning disabled" versus "People with learning disabilities are stupid"; "A physical disability may rule out a particular career option" versus "There are no worthwhile jobs for someone with a physical disability"; or "People are willing to accept me and my assets" versus "People only see my disability").

6. Teach the student to use positive self-talk to combat negative, irrational thoughts.

3. Design a plan for the current semester to improve academic performance and social interactions. (7, 8, 9, 10)

7. Encourage the student to discuss academic and social situations in which he/she was successful to identify personal strengths and increase his/her sense or self-efficacy.

8. Assist the student in identifying those academic and social problems that can be improved by using his/her current strengths and skill set as well as the situations that require the assistance of others.

9. Contract with the student to select and commit to specific academic/social skills and strategies that he/she can implement immediately (e.g., reviewing all syllabi and noting assignments on a calendar, creating and following a daily to-do list, participating in a study group, or joining a campus organization of interest); evaluate his/her progress weekly, reinforcing for success and redirecting failure.

10. Using the HOPE model (e.g., (**H**elp = What type of help is required; **O**bligations = What has to be done and what is needed to prepare for it; **P**lans = Provide a structure to keep the student moving in the direction of his/her plans and goals; **E**ncouragement = Be a positive force in the student's life—a cheerleader and ally); help the student identify situations in which he/she requires the assistance of others and/or specific accommodations to succeed.

4. Create a list of allies—individuals or groups—that will provide support and assistance in efforts to achieve academically and socially. (11, 12, 13)

11. Connect the student to the campus health center for answers to ongoing health concerns and/or medication management.

12. Refer the student to the coordinator of services for students with disabilities to manage tutoring needs, connect with support groups for people with disabilities, and/or provide environmental accommodations in residence halls, classrooms or meeting rooms.

13. Provide the student with information about and promote participation in at least one campus organization to enhance his/her opportunities to interact with peers socially.

5. Implement the use of self-advocacy skills with instructors. (14, 15, 16, 17)

14. Suggest that the student request meetings with each professor, prior to registration for classes, to determine the need for accommodations by discussing requirements, performance concerns, and particular challenges posed by the course.

15. Teach the student assertive communication techniques (e.g., using I statements; stating concerns specifically, behaviorally, and nonjudgmentally; and making clear, direct requests).

16. Role-play the student's meetings with faculty to help him/her become comfortable with discussing his/her disability in a clear and objective way as well as asking for specific, realistic accommodations.

6. Apply self-advocacy techniques in any situation in which specific accommodations would facilitate full participation. (18, 19, 20)

7. Implement healthy mood management techniques to improve interpersonal interactions and self-esteem. (21, 22, 23, 24, 25)

17. Monitor the student's progress by meeting with his/her faculty, providing encouragement, and nurturing his/her ability to self-advocate.

18. Help the student identify other areas in his/her life where self-advocacy might be useful (e.g., with doctors, family members, or student groups).

19. Assist the student in identifying the accommodations that would be helpful (e.g., moving a student organization's meeting room to a more accessible location, asking the bookstore to order books on tape, or requesting that a physician or other health-care professional keep family members informed through conference calls or e-mail); encourage him/her to script these requests to ensure all necessary points are covered.

20. Role-play the student's request for accommodations to increase his/her confidence in the ability to act as his/her own advocate.

21. For a two-week period, ask the student to use a journal or tape recorder to track moods, causes of mood changes, and any mood-enhancing techniques he/she regularly uses.

22. Investigate the student's use of alcohol/drugs and connect him/her to appropriate resources (e.g., chemical dependence treatment center, student health center, AA, or NA) if substance use/abuse is an issue.

23. Connect the student with his/her physician to determine whether medication would be useful to manage mood and/or pain.

24. Contract with the student, in consultation with the physician, to limit or abstain from substances other than prescribed medication.

25. Educate the student about mood changes and specific techniques for effective management (e.g., calling a supportive friend or relative, positive self-talk, reframing negative thoughts, involvement in activities that nurture and recharge, or joining a support group).

8. Increase involvement in social interactions to improve self-esteem and sense of connection. (26, 27, 28, 29)

26. Assist the student in evaluating current relationships, noting which people are positive and healthy forces in his/her life and which people leave him/her feeling negative and/or depressed.

27. Encourage the student to initiate connections with positive people by scheduling socialization time through activities such as a lunch date or study meeting.

28. Help the student identify opportunities to notice and be positive toward others to encourage reciprocal relationships.

29. Teach the student the maintenance of personal boundaries to limit interactions with negative people.

9. Increase social contact with positive and supportive family members. (30, 31, 32)

30. Assess the quality of communication that currently exists between the student and his/her family members.

31. Help the student determine the form and amount of communication that would keep him/her connected to family supports while maintaining appropriate boundaries needed to support development.

32. Monitor and reinforce the student's progress in establishing and/or maintaining supportive communication with his/her family.

10. Identify career goals and commit to a plan of action. (33, 34, 35)

33. Explore the student's career aspirations.

34. Provide an overview for the student of the career selection process, using *Job Search Handbook for People with Disabilities* (Ryan).

35. Refer the student to the campus career center for assessment, career information, and/or experiential options.

11. Effectively utilize the academic, social, and vocational resources offered on campus. (36, 37)

36. Monitor the student's movement toward goals on a weekly basis for one to two semesters to ensure academic and social progress.

37. Encourage the student's participation in volunteer activities, work on campus, and internships to support his/her social and vocational progress.

__. _____   __. _____

_____   _____

__. _____   __. _____

_____   _____

__. _____   __. _____

_____   _____

DIAGNOSTIC SUGGESTIONS:

Axis I:

315.00	Reading Disorder
315.1	Mathematics Disorder
315.2	Disorder of Written Expression
314.01	Attention-Deficit/Hyperactivity Disorder, Combined Type
314.00	Attention-Deficit/Hyperactivity Disorder, Predominantly Inattentive Type
312.34	Intermittent Explosive Disorder
305.00	Alcohol Abuse
305.20	Cannabis Abuse
294.9	Conduct Disorder NOS
V62.3	Academic Problem
V62.2	Occupational Problem
V62.89	Phase of Life Problem
V71.09	No Diagnosis
799.9	Diagnosis Deferred

_____   _____

_____   _____

Axis II:

301.50	Histrionic Personality Disorder
301.82	Avoidant Personality Disorder
301.9	Personality Disorder NOS
V71.09	No Diagnosis
799.9	Diagnosis Deferred

_____   _____

_____   _____

LONELINESS

BEHAVIORAL DEFINITIONS

1. Recent loss of a significant relationship (e.g., breakup with partner, death of family member, a transfer of a friend to another school) causes grief and withdrawal.
2. Suffers from social anxiety that inhibits building new relationships.
3. Feels sad, anxious, desperate, worthless, or isolated when alone.
4. Fills every possible moment with structured activity to avoid being alone.
5. Stays in his/her room rather than seeking opportunities to interact with peers.
6. Spends significant amount of time visiting home.
7. Focuses on maintaining friendships at home rather than building relationships at school.
8. Acts as if relationships at school are not important, refusing to reveal any feelings of vulnerability.
9. Alienates self from others through demanding and intrusive behavior.

___. _____
_____

___. _____
_____

___. _____
_____

LONG-TERM GOALS

1. Actively grieve recent or past losses.
2. Overcome social anxiety and become involved in campus opportunities for connection and support.
3. Recognize that developing and maintaining healthy relationships is a process requiring time, openness, and trust.
4. Replace the relationship dance (i.e., playing the pursuer or the pursued) with behaviors conducive to constructing a healthy relationship.
5. View time alone as an opportunity for self-knowledge and self-care.
6. Invest in relationships at school in addition to maintaining relationships at home.

—. _____
   _____
   _____
—. _____
   _____
   _____
—. _____
   _____

SHORT-TERM OBJECTIVES

THERAPEUTIC INTERVENTIONS

1. Discuss the current factors that contribute to and result from a lack of social network. (1, 2)

1. Ask the student to discuss as specifically as possible his/her perception of the causes for his/her loneliness (e.g., others are not friendly, roommate is distant, social anxiety inhibits reaching out to others, or too busy with studies to socialize).

2. Encourage the student to share the results of the lack of social network (e.g., rarely leaves his/her room; spends excessive amounts of time on the Internet, watching TV, or playing video games; or stays overinvolved and excessively busy).

2. Identify the thoughts and feelings associated with loneliness. (3, 4)

3. Explore the feelings underlying the student's loneliness (e.g., grief, fear, anxiety, desperation, or depression).

4. Assign a journal in which the student can express his/her feelings and their associated thoughts or beliefs (be alert for cognitive distortions).

3. Identify and replace the cognitive distortions that maintain the social withdrawal. (5, 6, 7)

5. Help the student to write a list of the beliefs that are at the root of his/her present loneliness.

6. Assist the student in evaluating his/her beliefs for cognitive distortions (e.g., "I will be alone forever"; "If I allow myself to feel the pain of loosing my father, it will kill me"; or "If I reach out, I will be rejected").

7. Reframe the student's cognitive distortions about socialization (e.g., "There's no point in going out because no one will talk to me" versus "If I go out, I can begin conversations with people that seem interesting"; "If I end this relationship now I won't get hurt" versus "If I get hurt, I will survive and hopefully learn something to make the next relationship better"; "He/she would never be interested in spending time with me" versus "I need to stop reading minds and negatively predicting the future").

4. Identify any personal history that offers insight into the impact of loneliness on self-esteem. (8, 9, 10, 11)

8. Support the student as he/she identifies other times of extreme loneliness in his/her life.

9. Request that the student share his/her reactions to previous times of loneliness and help

him/her recognize dysfunctional patterns of behavior (e.g., distancing from or clinging to others, pushing others away and then feeling angry when they leave, or ignoring losses by being "fine").

10. Explore the effects of the student's dysfunctional social behavior on his/her self-esteem (e.g., believing himself/herself to be unlovable, feeling fatally flawed in some way, or seeing himself/herself as doomed to be alone forever).

11. Investigate the effects of the student's dysfunctional social behaviors on his/her current situation and on his/her ability to connect with others in a healthy way on campus (e.g., diminished capacity to reach out, trust, be vulnerable, or allow individuation).

5. Grieve losses in healthy, constructive ways. (12, 13)

12. Educate the student on the stages of the grieving process, assuring him/her of his/her ability to survive it (see Grief/Loss chapter in this *Planner*).

13. Suggest that the student take advantage of campus support groups.

6. Verbalize an understanding that ricocheting between attempts to distance from and attempts to hold on to another usually result in the loss of that relationship. (14, 15, 16)

14. Help the student understand the components of the relationship dance (e.g., fear of being abandoned or enmeshed) as defined in *The Dance of Intimacy* (Lerner).

15. Explain to the student the concept that differentiation in healthy relationships is the

ability to allow for connection to another as well as the ability to remain whole and complete as an individual.

16. Using the concepts of the relationship dance and relationship differentiation, encourage the student to evaluate current and past losses to determine his/her role in the demise of his/her relationships.

7. Implement anxiety coping skills necessary to participate in and enjoy a range of relationships. (17, 18, 19)

17. Teach the student to stop dancing by recognizing the feelings and/or situations that trigger his/her need to cling or push away.

18. Coach the student on the use of quick techniques (e.g., deep breathing, thought stopping, or positive self-talk, affirmations) to manage the immediate anxiety that he/she will experience when he/she refrains from running away from or clinging to a relationship.

19. Recommend that the student read material on overcoming social anxiety (e.g., *Overcoming Social Anxiety & Shyness* by Butler and *The Shyness and Social Anxiety Workbook: Proven Techniques for Overcoming Your Fears* by Antony and Swinson); process the implementation of concepts learned.

8. Reduce the anxiety produced by being alone. (20, 21)

20. Discuss the difference between loneliness and being alone (e.g., *loneliness:* a disquieting sense of isolation; a feeling of sadness or despair because of a lack of friendship or companionship

that can be experienced while alone or with others; *being alone:* a physical state of being separate, apart, or solitary that can be peaceful, relaxing, and/or rejuvenating) with the student.

21. Encourage the student to use anxiety-management techniques to cope with the initial anxiety he/she will feel when alone.

9. Report on the positive use of alone time. (22, 23, 24)

22. Cultivate the student's ability to be alone by asking him/her to use poster paper to create a list of satisfying alone-time activity options (e.g., reading, writing, drawing or painting, listening to music, walking, watching a favorite video, or playing with a pet).

23. Ask the student to include at least 30 minutes of alone time in his/her daily schedule to be comfortable with and eventually welcome these moments.

24. Track the student's progress in developing a comfort level with alone time at weekly meetings, reinforcing success and redirecting failure.

10. Participate in campus services, groups, and organizations to feel a part of campus life. (25, 26, 27, 28)

25. Invite the student to review a list of campus organizations or clubs (found in the student handbook or at the campus activities office) and identify several to consider for his/her involvement.

26. Encourage the student to write campus events of interest in his/her calendar and to attend at least one event each week.

27. Suggest that the student attend a few meetings of each organization of interest and select one or two in which to participate.

28. Refer the student to the campus recreation facility to investigate classes or intramural teams and register for at least one.

11. Acknowledge that loneliness will occur at various points in life but does not have to be devastating and can be managed. (29, 30)

29. Continue to meet weekly with the student for a semester to track his/her participation in campus life, reinforcing success and redirecting failure.

30. Continue to support the student in developing his/her own interests and relationships and in managing loneliness when it surfaces.

__. _____   __. _____
    _____   _____

__. _____   __. _____
    _____   _____

__. _____   __. _____
    _____   _____

DIAGNOSTIC SUGGESTIONS:

Axis I: 300.4   Dysthymic Disorder
              308.3   Acute Stress Disorder
              300.02   Generalized Anxiety Disorder
              309.xx   Adjustment Disorder
              296.2x   Major Depressive Disorder, Single Episode
              V62.3   Academic Problem
              V62.89   Phase of Life Problem
              V71.09   No Diagnosis
              799.9   Diagnosis Deferred

_____   _____

_____   _____

Axis II: 301.6   Dependent Personality Disorder
301.83   Borderline Personality Disorder
V71.09   No Diagnosis
799.9   Diagnosis Deferred

_____   _____

_____   _____

PREGNANCY

BEHAVIORAL DEFINITIONS

1. Has become pregnant within the context of a long-term relationship.
2. Has become pregnant within the context of a new relationship or a sexual encounter.
3. Experiences feelings of anxiety, embarrassment, and shame about the pregnancy.
4. Experiences conflicts with partner regarding choices about the pregnancy.
5. Is ambivalent about terminating the pregnancy.
6. Lacks information on how to safely implement the decision to terminate the pregnancy.
7. Desires to complete the pregnancy are accompanied by feelings of confusion and anxiety about the future.
8. Denies the implications of the pregnancy on current and future life and educational plans.
9. Lacks support systems to provide guidance and assistance during the pregnancy.
10. Decides to release the infant for adoption but lacks information on the process.
11. Withdraws from school because of the pregnancy.
12. Experiences significant conflict with family because of the pregnancy.

Some material in this chapter was adapted from the Teen Pregnancy chapter in *The Social Work and Human Services Treatment Planner* by J. Wodarski, L. A. Rapp-Paglicci, C. N. Dulmus, and A. E. Jongsma (New York: John Wiley & Sons, 2001). © 2001 by John Wodarski, Lisa A. Rapp-Paglicci, Catherine N. Dulmus, and Arthur E. Jongsma, Jr. Reprinted with permission.

__·__ _____
_____
__·__ _____
_____
__·__ _____
_____

LONG-TERM GOALS

1. Make a decision about the completion or termination of the pregnancy.
2. Complete abortion if termination is selected.
3. Obtain ongoing prenatal care if completion is selected.
4. Make the choice to keep the child or to release the infant for adoption.
5. Create and follow through on a plan to continue education.
6. Encourage the support of family by maintaining ongoing communication and providing information about pregnancy decisions.
7. Use effective forms of birth control after the pregnancy.

__·__ _____
_____
__·__ _____
_____
__·__ _____
_____

SHORT-TERM OBJECTIVES

THERAPEUTIC INTERVENTIONS

1. Confirm the pregnancy and its duration. (1)

1. Refer the student to the student health center for testing to confirm the pregnancy and its duration.

2. Identify the facts and feelings about the pregnancy. (2, 3, 4)

2. Explore the relationship circumstance leading to and the student's feelings about the pregnancy.

3. Examine the current stability and possible future of the

3. List the pregnancy response
   options and the expected
   consequences of each potential
   response. (5, 6)

4. Make a decision about
   completing or terminating the
   pregnancy. (6, 7, 8)

relationship with his/her partner
in the pregnancy with the
student.

4. Investigate the family dynamics
   that may have contributed to
   the student's behavior (e.g.,
   rejection or abandonment
   issues, sexual abuse history, or
   modeling of casual attitudes
   about sexual intimacy).

5. Assist the student in evaluating
   the range of options for the
   pregnancy (i.e., abortion,
   adoption, or keeping the baby).

6. Teach the student problem-
   solving techniques (e.g.,
   brainstorming options, analyzing
   the pros and cons of each option
   generated, utilizing outside
   resources to review options,
   and reality test) that can apply to
   this situation to improve his/her
   decision making.

6. Teach the student problem-
   solving techniques (e.g.,
   brainstorming options, analyzing
   the pros and cons of each option
   generated, utilizing outside
   resources to review options,
   and reality test) that can
   apply to this situation to
   improve his/her decision
   making.

7. Conduct a session with the
   couple, including both of the
   partners in the problem-solving
   process as appropriate.

8. Encourage the student to
   contact family members,
   apprising them of the situation
   and discussing the ways in
   which they can provide support.

5. Access a range of campus services to aid in coping with the stress of the pregnancy and related decisions. (9, 10)

6. Access medical and prenatal care on a consistent basis. (11)

7. Continue progress toward academic goals. (12, 13, 14)

8. Agree to attend parenting education classes. (15)

9. Verbalize realistic expectations for life after delivery. (15, 16, 17, 18)

9. Continue individual and/or couples counseling about the implementation and effects of the pregnancy-related decisions.

10. Refer the student to a campus therapy group to increase affective outlets and sources of support.

11. Refer the student to the campus health center for medical and prenatal care.

12. Reinforce the student's class attendance and completion of assignments.

13. Encourage the student to alert instructors and/or the dean's office if special arrangements are necessary because of medical/prenatal concerns.

14. Refer the student to an academic advisor to discuss schedule changes and their impact on graduation and career goals.

15. Provide parenting education or refer the student to a campus or community resource.

15. Provide parenting education or refer the student to a campus or community resource.

16. Assist the student in setting realistic postpregnancy goals that consider the responsibilities of caring for a child.

17. Review all potential sources of emotional and child care support after the delivery with the student.

18. Assist the student in evaluating and choosing an alternative living arrangement for

subsequent semesters if currently living in the residence halls.

10. Agree to consistently use birth control postpregnancy. (19)

19. Discuss the importance of using birth control postpregnancy and refer the student to the health center, Planned Parenthood, or other resources that provide access to birth control measures.

11. Verbalize a decision for abortion or release of parental rights that is free of guilt. (20, 21, 22, 23)

20. Explore the student's moral, religious, cultural, and ethnic values about abortion or adoption for possible conflicts; reinforce his/her right to make an informed decision about the pregnancy.

21. Prepare the student for the range of emotions that accompany an abortion or adoption decision (e.g., shame, guilt, sadness, anger, or loneliness) and encourage him/her to verbalize these feelings to resolve them.

22. Support the student in coping with attitudes of family and friends about the pregnancy decision.

23. Meet weekly with the student for a full semester post-pregnancy to provide encouragement and identify resources for practical assistance as necessary.

__. _____   __. _____
   _____   _____
__. _____   __. _____
   _____   _____
__. _____   __. _____
   _____   _____

DIAGNOSTIC SUGGESTIONS:

Axis I:	308.3	Acute Stress Disorder
	309.0	Adjustment Disorder with Depressed Mood
	309.24	Adjustment Disorder with Anxiety
	309.28	Adjustment Disorder with Mixed Anxiety and Depressed Mood
	300.00	Anxiety Disorder NOS
	V62.89	Phase of Life Problem
	V71.09	No Diagnosis
	799.9	Diagnosis Deferred
	_____	_____
	_____	_____
Axis II:	V71.09	No Diagnosis
	799.9	Diagnosis Deferred
	_____	_____
	_____	_____

PSYCHOTIC BREAK

BEHAVIORAL DEFINITIONS

1. Verbalizes bizarre thoughts (e.g., delusions of grandeur, persecution, reference, influence, control, somatic sensations, and/or infidelity).
2. Presents with highly illogical forms of thoughts/speech (e.g., loose association of ideas in speech; incoherence; illogical thinking; vague, abstract, or repetitive speech; neologisms; perseverations; or clanging).
3. Verbalizes evidence of worsening perceptual disturbances (e.g., hallucinations, primarily auditory but occasionally visual or olfactory).
4. Demonstrates seriously disturbed affect (e.g., blunted, none, flattened, or inappropriate).
5. Exhibits a loss of a sense of self (e.g., loss of ego boundaries, lack of identity, or blatant confusion).
6. Demonstrates greatly diminished volition (e.g., inadequate interest, drive, or ability to follow a course of action to its logical conclusion; pronounced ambivalence or cessation of goal-directed activity; missed classes; or lack of participation in academic activities and extra-curriculars).
7. Substantially withdraws from relationships (withdrawal from involvement with external world, preoccupation with egocentric ideas and fantasies, alienation from roommates, classmates, friends, and/or family).
8. Exhibits persistent psychomotor abnormalities (marked decrease in reactivity to campus/external environment; various catatonic patterns, such as stupor, rigidity, excitement, posturing, or negativism; or unusual mannerisms or grimacing).
9. Is acutely unable to adequately care for own physical needs, which is potentially harmful to self.

—. _____
_____
_____

—. _____
_____
_____

—. _____
_____

LONG-TERM GOALS

1. Eliminate acute, reactive, psychotic symptoms and return to normal functioning in affect, thinking, and relating.
2. Stabilize functioning adequately to allow return to productive and satisfying academic life and campus activities.
3. Take psychotropic medication consistently.
4. Reduce significantly or eliminate hallucinations and/or delusions.
5. Develop adaptive methods to cope with symptoms and seek treatment when necessary.

—. _____
_____
_____

—. _____
_____
_____

—. _____
_____

SHORT-TERM OBJECTIVES

1. Describe the thoughts, feelings, and perceptions that are interfering with normal functioning on campus. (1, 2, 3)

THERAPEUTIC INTERVENTIONS

1. Actively build a level of trust with the student using consistent eye contact, active listening, unconditional positive regard, and warm acceptance to help increase his/her ability to identifying and expressing symptoms.

2. Explore the student's irrational beliefs and assess the content for

themes or patterns to better structure treatment and set goals.

3. Evaluate the severity of the student's reality perception disturbance and the frequency of intrusive irrational thoughts.

2. Clarify the history of the development of psychotic symptoms. (4, 5)

4. Explore the student's process of symptom development from the past through the present; determine whether his/her psychosis is acute, reactive, or chronic with prodromal and reactive elements.

5. Explore the student's family history for evidence of serious mental illness.

3. Describe recent perceived severe stressors at school that may have precipitated this acute psychotic break. (4, 6)

4. Explore the student's process of symptom development from the past through the present; determine whether his/her psychosis is acute, reactive, or chronic with prodromal and reactive elements.

6. Probe the causes for the student's reactive psychosis; evaluate the nature and severity of stressors that may have triggered the psychotic break.

4. Cooperate with psychological testing to evaluate thought-disturbance severity. (7)

7. Perform or refer the student for psychological testing to evaluate the pervasiveness of the thought disturbance; report the results to him/her and/or to the family and consulting professionals after appropriate consent has been obtained.

5. Cooperate with a psychiatric evaluation to assess the need for antipsychotic medication and to evaluate/rule out brain tumors, dementia, or other

8. Refer the student to a psychiatrist to evaluate his/her need for antipsychotic medication and to provide a physical examination to evaluate/rule out any organic

contributing/casual organic factors. (8)

6. Verbalize an understanding of the need for and comply with consistently taking anti-psychotic medication as prescribed, and report on the efficacy and side effects. (9, 10)

7. Take a hiatus from school to live in a supervised environment and/or psychiatric hospital. (11, 12, 13)

8. Verbalize an understanding that the distressing symptoms are due to a mental illness. (14, 15, 16)

factors that may be contributory/causal to the psychotic symptoms.

9. Monitor the student's compliance with medication, noting efficacy and any side effects; collaborate with the prescribing psychiatrist after obtaining his/her consent for release of information.

10. Educate the student about the use and expected benefits of psychotropic medications.

11. Collaborate with psychiatrist, family, and the student to evaluate whether he/she needs to be hospitalized psychiatrically.

12. Help with making arrangements for the student to take a hiatus from school and live under the supervision of his/her family.

13. Make arrangements for involuntary commitment to an inpatient psychiatric facility if the student is unable to care for his/her basic needs or is harmful to him/herself or others and is uncooperative with voluntary admission.

14. Explain the nature of the psychotic process, its biochemical component, and its confusing effect on rational thought.

15. Assist in identifying distorted perceptions of reality and replace with actual, reality-based understandings; use role-play and modeling to teach the application of analyzing a situation and considering more rational implications.

16. Provide supportive therapy to alleviate the student's fears and reduce feelings of alienation.

9. Utilize various media to express identified feelings of alienation, fear, and isolation. (17)

17. Conduct art therapy and encourage the student to express feelings through various art media; discuss the meaning of the artwork.

10. Demonstrate a reduction in thought disturbance by reporting less frequent and less severe hallucinations and the cessation of delusions. (9, 18, 19, 20)

9. Monitor the student's compliance with medication, noting efficacy and any side effects; collaborate with the prescribing psychiatrist after obtaining his/her consent for release of information.

18. Gently provide the student with alternative, reality-based perceptions when hallucinations are described.

19. Encourage the focus on the reality of the external world versus the student's disoriented and distorted perceptions and beliefs.

20. Calmly and matter-of-factly confront the student's delusional thoughts, offering reality-based explanations or interpretations without debate.

11. Report and demonstrate the cessation of bizarre behaviors. (9, 21)

9. Monitor the student's compliance with medication, noting efficacy and any side effects; collaborate with the prescribing psychiatrist after obtaining his/her consent for release of information.

21. Positively reinforce the student for normal appearance, behavior, and/or speech (e.g., terminate talking to self, laughing or crying inappropriately, posturing, facial

grimaces, incoherent speech, or blank staring).

12. Identify and replace distorted self-talk that precipitates disturbing emotions. (22, 23)

22. Assist the student in identifying his/her negative, distorted self-talk that precipitates or mediates symptoms and emotional upset.

23. Teach the student realistic, positive self-talk to increase his/her sense of reality.

13. Identify and replace irrational beliefs with reality-based perceptions. (24, 25)

24. Assist the student in identifying his/her irrational beliefs that act as barriers to accurately understanding reality.

25. Teach the student to rationally reframe his/her irrational beliefs.

14. Identify a support system in the residence-hall environment that will encourage and assist in managing stresses and seek help if needed. (26, 27)

26. Explore peer resources (e.g., study groups, low-key social functions, or peer-lead education groups on managing college stressors) available to the student for dealing with stressors.

27. Assist the student in identifying administrative staff that may be available (e.g., resident advisor or residence director) to provide him/her with suggestions or support when needed.

15. Engage in social interactions that are reality-based, coherent, subject focused, logical, organized, and characterized by appropriate affect. (28, 29)

28. Role-play and/or conduct role-reversal with various social interactions and give the student feedback on the appropriateness of his/her social skills.

29. Positively reinforce the student's initiation of appropriate social interactions with roommates, friends, other students, and faculty.

16. Attend properly to basic needs of dress, hygiene, grooming, and toileting. (21, 30)

21. Positively reinforce the student for normal appearance, behavior, and/or speech (e.g., terminate talking to self, laughing or crying

inappropriately, posturing, facial grimaces, incoherent speech, or blank staring).

30. Assign the student the task of preparing a daily list of self-care activities; positively reinforce independent performance of the activities of daily living.

17. Sleep in a normal pattern of six to nine hours per night without agitation, fear, or disruption. (31)

31. Direct the student to sleep at expected times and positively reinforce him/her for compliance.

18. Family members verbalize an understanding that the bizarre behavior and irrational thoughts experienced by the student are due to a mental illness. (32, 33, 34, 35)

32. Hold family therapy sessions to replace an atmosphere of criticism or hostility toward the student with compassion, empathy, and support for him/her; educate the family about the symptoms of mental illness, emphasizing the nonvolitional aspects of psychosis.

33. Arrange for family therapy meetings/sessions to provide information about the student's treatment and prognosis.

34. Encourage family members to share their feelings of frustration, guilt, fear, or grief about the student's mental illness and/or behavior patterns (without the student present).

35. Assist the family in replacing any double-binding messages, which are inconsistent and contradictory and result in the student's increased anxiety, confusion, and/or psychotic symptoms, with clear, direct, concrete, and supportive communication.

19. Verbalize an awareness of indicators of decompensation

36. Teach the student to recognize critical symptoms that are

and methods to contact the therapist, roommate, and/or family/significant other if problems worsen. (36, 37)

20. Take steps to change the student's environment to reduce the feelings of threat associated with it. (12, 26, 27, 38, 39)

indicative of decompensation, urging him/her to initiate clinical contact if these symptoms of psychosis appear and begin to interfere with his/her daily functioning; inform his/her roommate, friends, and/or family members of this plan for early intervention after obtaining appropriate consent.

37. Provide the family, roommates, friends, and student with written instructions and telephone numbers to use if his/her symptoms intensify.

12. Help with making arrangements for the student to take a hiatus from school and live under the supervision of his/her family.

26. Explore peer resources (e.g., study groups, low-key social functions, or peer-lead education groups on managing college stressors) available to the student for dealing with stressors.

27. Assist the student in identifying administrative staff that may be available (e.g., resident advisor or residence director) to provide him/her with suggestions or support when needed.

38. Assist the student in identifying stressors that may have triggered his/her psychotic episode (e.g., social isolation, academic pressure, roommate conflict, absence from home and family, substance abuse, romantic rejection).

39. Address each trigger to identify steps to take to reduce the stress in the student's life.

21. Gradually return to classes and the academic setting at a functional level similar to the premorbid level and accept the responsibility of caring for his/her basic needs. (29, 40)

29. Positively reinforce the student's initiation of appropriate social interactions with roommates, friends, other students, and faculty.

40. Arrange for the student to return to a reduced number of academic classes, informing the faculty (after obtaining consent) of his/her serious mental illness issues; monitor and support the resumption of responsibilities.

__. _____   __. _____
    _____   _____
__. _____   __. _____
    _____   _____
__. _____   __. _____
    _____   _____

DIAGNOSTIC SUGGESTIONS:

Axis I:

297.1	Delusional Disorder
298.8	Brief Psychotic Disorder
295.xx	Schizophrenia
295.30	Schizophrenia, Paranoid Type
295.70	Schizoaffective Disorder
295.40	Schizophreniform Disoder
296.xx	Bipolar I Disorder
296.89	Bipolar II Disorder
296.24	Major Depressive Disorder, Single Episode, Severe with Psychotic Features
310.1	Personality Change Due to (Axis III Disorder)

_____ _____
_____ _____

Axis II:

799.9	Diagnosis Deferred
V71.09	No Diagnosis

_____ _____
_____ _____

RAPE/SEXUAL ASSAULT VICTIM

BEHAVIORAL DEFINITIONS

1. Experiences persistent somatic problems (e.g., insomnia, nightmares, exaggerated startle response, headaches, stomach and/or back pain, or skin problems).
2. Feels vulnerable and powerless, resulting in confusion, inability to concentrate, indecisiveness, fear, panic reactions, and/or phobias.
3. Thinks and talks obsessively about the assault.
4. Refuses to acknowledge that the assault occurred and/or its impact on normal functioning.
5. Believes common myths about victims of rape and sexual assault (e.g., they ask for it, enjoy it, could have fought harder, bring it on themselves by the way they dress or act, or were too drunk to say, "No" so its their own fault).
6. Believes common myths about perpetrators of rape and sexual assault (e.g., they are obviously crazy and deranged, or they are strangers who can't control themselves).
7. Experiences feelings of self-blame and shame about the assault that result in social isolation, depression, irritability, mood swings, or dangerous behavior
8. Is overwhelmed by anger toward the perpetrator and anguish about the assault.
9. Demonstrates failed or diminished performance of daily academic tasks (e.g., attending classes, completing assignment, or taking tests).
10. Only sporadically accomplishes the tasks of daily living (e.g., bathing, cleaning clothes and living space, or eating).

—. _____

_____

—. _____

_____

—. _____

_____

LONG-TERM GOALS

1. Effectively manage the fears and feelings associated with sexual assault to feel some sense of safety and control over life.
2. Practice the behaviors necessary to heal from rape/sexual assault, recognizing that recovery is a process that may last for months.
3. Accept that rape/sexual assault is never the victim's fault.
4. Understand that the physical and psychosocial changes experienced as a result of the sexual assault are normal reactions to a traumatizing event.
5. Learn and practice rape and sexual assault prevention techniques.
6. Create an outlook that recognizes the impact of this trauma while integrating it into a larger sense of identity and purpose as a survivor.

—. _____

_____

—. _____

_____

—. _____

_____

SHORT-TERM OBJECTIVES

1. Verbalize a feeling of safety within the counseling environment. (1, 2)

THERAPEUTIC INTERVENTIONS

1. Encourage the student to select a comfortable seat or rearrange the seating so that he/she feels safe in the environment; reassure him/her that you want to do everything possible to enhance his/her feelings of safety and security.

2. Stock the office with items that can offer a sense of security (e.g., pillows, a throw, or stuffed animals) and encourage the student to hold them if they provide some comfort.

2. Provide as much information as possible about the rape/sexual assault. (3, 4, 5)

3. Ask the student to talk about the circumstances surrounding his/her rape/sexual assault (e.g., when, where, who, or activities prior to assault).

4. Encourage the student to offer as much information as possible about the assault itself (e.g., what was done, threats, feelings, who was notified, rape kit done, or charges filed).

5. Name the act for the student as *rape* or *sexual assault* and provide him/her with clear definitions (*rape:* sexual intercourse, sodomy, or oral copulation accomplished against a person's will; or *sexual assault:* any sexual act committed or attempted against a person's will.)

3. Verbalize the feelings evoked by the rape/sexual assault. (6, 7, 8, 9)

6. Clarify the range of feelings that this type of trauma elicits (e.g., emotional numbness and shock, shame and guilt, disbelief and denial, powerlessness and fear, anxiety and depression, or anger and anguish) for the student.

7. Help the student to identify, verbalize, and normalize as specifically as possible his/ her own feelings about the rape/sexual assault.

8. Encourage the student to record feelings and thoughts in a daily journal to document and provide

4. Verbalize a factual understanding of rape/sexual assault
that exposes common myths.
(10, 11, 12)

5. Obtain medical care to treat
rape-related concerns.
(13, 14, 15)

a release for feelings; ask
him/her to bring the journal to
sessions for a review.

9. Prepare the student for the
possibility that a flood of
feelings may be triggered
without warning at various times
and reassure him/her that these
feelings are not a precursor to
"going crazy."

10. Support the student in sharing
his/her own beliefs about
rape/sexual assault to determine
whether he/she is operating
under any myths or irrational
beliefs.

11. Reinforce several key concepts:
(a) rape/sexual assault is never
the fault of the victim; (b) it may
be difficult to talk about the
assault, but talking will help you
heal; (c) having difficulty with
this trauma does not mean that
you are not handling things well;
(d) denial or refusal to deal with
what happened does not move
you toward the goal of "getting
on with your life"; and (e) while
this trauma will disrupt your life
for a while, you will eventually
heal and regain a sense of
equilibrium as a survivor.

12. Suggest that the student read *I
Never Called It Rape* (Warshaw)
or *Against Our Will: Women,
Men and Rape* (Brownmiller) to
reinforce factual information
about rape.

13. Inquire about the emergency
medical treatment that the
student received immediately
following the assault.

14. Refer the student to the campus health center to follow up on any medical concerns resulting from the rape/sexual assault.

15. Assure the student of your support through any medical and legal processes that he/she undertakes.

6. Follow through on filing a police report and charges against the sexual offender. (15, 16, 17)

15. Assure the student of your support through any medical and legal processes that he/she undertakes.

16. Inquire about the student's contact with police and/or legal counsel following the assault to report the assailant and file charges.

17. Offer referrals to the campus public safety office, the campus legal clinic, or community law enforcement and legal resources if a report was not filed.

7. Identify and implement behaviors that will create a sense of safety. (18, 19, 20)

18. Encourage the student to meet at least twice a week for counseling during the initial phase of recovery to receive ongoing support and guidance.

19. Brainstorm a list of safety measures that the student could put into place immediately (e.g., staying with a friend for a few days, always using the campus escort service, changing locks, or buy a dog) to enhance feelings of security.

20. Suggest that the student register for a self-defense class (typically offered by the community or campus public safety department or the campus sports center).

8. Implement anxiety- and stress-management techniques. (21, 22, 23, 24)

21. Connect the student with a trainer from the campus recreation center to develop a workout routine that will alleviate stress.

22. Encourage the student to join an intramural sports team or club to keep physically active and connected to others.

23. Help the student develop a list of relaxation techniques that he/she will try (e.g., yoga, deep muscle relaxation, massage, music, hot baths, or meditation).

24. Focus the student on the importance of maintaining a balanced diet and routine sleep cycle during recovery; refer him/her to a nutritionist at the campus health center if necessary.

9. Share the assault experience with people who can be supportive of the healing process. (25, 26, 27, 28)

25. Assist the student in identifying people who can be supportive and nonjudgmental as he/she goes through the recovery process.

26. Role-play a conversation in which the student talks about the assault and asks for specific types of support while also setting boundaries.

27. Review the student's efforts and provide support as he/she makes contact with family and friends to tell them what occurred and asks for their help.

28. Refer the student to campus support groups that fit his/her recovery process.

10. Review current academic situation and make decisions

29. Ask the student to identify current academic concerns (e.g.,

that support both academic success and the recovery process. (29, 30, 31, 32)

missed classes, assignments, or tests) and determine the best approach for dealing with class requirements.

30. Outline academic options for classes where too much has been missed (e.g., contact the campus health center to arrange for a medical release; the academic dean to arrange withdrawal from classes; or academic advisors or professors to arrange extensions or incompletes).

31. Offer, with the student's permission, to discuss selected options with necessary college personnel to determine the information and documentation required of the student.

32. Provide the student with the names of individuals he/she must contact and the exact information that he/she must provide.

11. Use a journal as a continued source of information on feelings and fears that must be dealt with for healing to occur. (8, 33, 34, 35)

8. Encourage the student to record feelings and thoughts in a daily journal to document and provide a release for feelings; ask him/her to bring the journal to sessions for a review.

33. Process particular issues and patterns that are evident from the student's journal entries, focusing on the use of specific techniques to deal with fear, anger, and/or grief (e.g., sexual dysfunction, social isolation, or distancing/disengaging from intimate relationships).

34. Suggest that the student write a letter to or role-play a meeting with the perpetrator to direct his/her anger at the appropriate

target if anger is a particular concern.

35. Gently encourage the student to allow his/her sadness or anger to surface, reminding him/her that these overwhelming feelings will end and he/she will not cry forever or be consumed by the anger.

12. Incorporate rest and play as integral parts of daily living. (36, 37)

36. Encourage the student to take time outs (e.g., quiet times to relax, nap, or read).

37. Help the student recognize that engaging in play time is essential to healing and assist him/her identify activities that are fun (e.g., playing an instrument, painting, gardening, or crafts); monitor and reinforce this distracting, relaxing activity.

13. Identify and implement safety-enhancing daily practices. (38, 39, 40)

38. Assist the student in attaining a heightened awareness of the surroundings (e.g., park in lighted areas, always lock room and car doors, avoid isolated places day or night, know the location of emergency phones on campus).

39. Support the student in listening to his/her instincts (e.g., if you believe there is something wrong, there probably is—even if you can't specifically identify it).

40. Develop a safety checklist (e.g., remember the disinhibiting impact of alcohol and drugs, meet someone for the first time in a public place, don't bring someone home whom you have just met, don't walk alone, don't prop outside doors open, and don't let someone into your

14. Actively participate in the recovery process until a sense of control and equilibrium in life is regained. (41)

building if they don't have a key) with the student that can be posted and read daily.

41. Meet weekly with the student for approximately six months after the rape/sexual assault to process all emotions, provide guidance in getting day-to-day living back on track, and manage any ongoing concerns and fallout from the trauma; after six months, monitor the recovery process on a bi-weekly basis until he/she is prepared for and comfortable with his/her own life again.

__. _____   __. _____
    _____   _____
__. _____   __. _____
    _____   _____
__. _____   __. _____
    _____   _____

DIAGNOSTIC SUGGESTIONS:

Axis I:	308.3	Acute Stress Disorder
	300.00	Anxiety Disorder NOS
	309.24	Adjustment Disorder with Anxiety
	309.0	Adjustment Disorder with Depressed Mood
	309.81	Posttraumatic Stress Disorder
	V71.09	No Diagnosis
	799.9	Diagnosis Deferred
	_____	_____
	_____	_____
Axis II:	301.9	Personality Disorder NOS
	V71.09	No Diagnosis
	799.9	Diagnosis Deferred
	_____	_____
	_____	_____

ROOMMATE CONFLICTS

BEHAVIORAL DEFINITIONS

1. Has frequent or ongoing disagreements (expressed or unexpressed) with another resident over one or several topics related to living together.
2. Verbally and/or nonverbally hostile toward a roommate.
3. Attempts to resolve conflicts with a roommate are consistently unsuccessful.
4. Feels anxious and angry when in contact with the disliked roommate.
5. Has conflict with the roommate due to clashing personality styles (e.g., quiet versus loud, assertive versus passive, extravert versus introvert, or leader versus leader).
6. Has conflict with the roommate due to clashing values and priorities (e.g., studying versus partying, sleep versus socializing, or cleanliness versus sloppiness).
7. Experiences stress, sleep disturbance, concentration loss, and lower academic performance due to roommate conflicts.
8. Projects responsibility for the conflict almost solely onto the roommate.
9. Lacks problem-solving and assertiveness skills.
10. Lacks social skills for building and maintaining a broad social network.

—. _____
   _____

—. _____
   _____

—. _____
   _____

LONG-TERM GOALS

1. Resolve interpersonal conflicts with roommates.
2. Develop conflict-management skills to enhance the possibility of negotiating win-win solutions to interpersonal problems.
3. Develop assertive communication skills to improve the ability to recognize and affirm another roommate's point of view and to interact directly and respectfully.
4. Improve living in community through enhanced communication and self-awareness.

—. _____

   _____

—. _____

   _____

—. _____

   _____

SHORT-TERM OBJECTIVES

THERAPEUTIC INTERVENTIONS

1. Tell the complete story of the roommate conflict. (1, 2)

1. Explore the student's history and nature of disagreements with people with whom he/she lives; encourage him/her to discuss the conflicts in specific behavioral terms rather than global generalizations.

2. Assist the student in exploring and clarifying his/her feelings about the disagreements with roommates.

2. Identify typical emotional and behavioral responses to inter-personal conflict situations. (3, 4)

3. Assist the student in identifying and listing his/her typical behavioral responses to the interpersonal conflict.

4. Help the student recognize, express, and list his/her typical feeling responses to the interpersonal conflict.

3. Examine ways in which conflict is managed in the family of origin to identify learned responses to conflict, anger, and anxiety. (5, 6, 7)

4. Identify changes in behavior that would help reduce tension and improve living conditions (8, 9)

5. Explore the student's family of origin to identify dysfunctional patterns of conflict resolution (e.g., projection of all responsibility for conflict onto others, angry aggressive reactions, or withdrawal and poor communication).

6. Assign the student homework of writing a summary of the last three arguments or conflicts that occurred at home, including each family member's reaction and how the conflict was resolved; process the assignment results for learned patterns of conflict management in the family.

7. Assist the student in understanding the link between his/her family's dysfunctional and ineffective conflict management patterns and his/her current pattern of responding to roommate conflicts.

8. Assist the student in creating a list of general conflict responses that are useful to effective conflict management (e.g., staying calm and quiet, using I messages and active listening skills, acknowledging his/her own role, or examining many possible solutions).

9. Compare the list of the student's behavioral and emotional responses to conflict to the list of effective conflict management responses, noting the student's areas that need improvement to develop effective conflict management skills (e.g., need to learn relaxation, active listening,

assertiveness, or problem-
solving skills).

5. Implement specific behavioral responses to conflict to improve direct and respectful communication. (10, 11, 12, 13)

10. Introduce the student to a model for assertive dialog that respectfully identifies issues in behavioral terms, recognizes both individuals' needs and rights, and offers possible solutions that are mutually beneficial.

11. Teach the student effective conflict resolution or problem-solving skills: (a) problem identification or clarification in behavioral terms; (b) mutual brainstorming of possible alternative solutions and review of the pros and cons of each; (c) mutual selection of an alternative solution for implementation; (d) evaluation of the outcome in terms of mutual satisfaction; and (e) adjustment of the solution, if necessary, to increase mutual satisfaction.

12. Use role-play and modeling to teach the application of effective conflict resolution techniques to the student's current issues of disagreement with his/her roommate.

13. Assign the student the task of selecting a conflict with a roommate and implementing the new resolution skills he/she has learned; process the results of the encounter, reinforcing success and redirecting failure.

6. Identify and replace distorted self-talk that precipitates disturbing emotions during conflict resolution. (14, 15)

14. Assist the student in identifying his/her negative, distorted self-talk that precipitates or mediates feelings of anger, anxiety, dis-

trust, or defensiveness (e.g., "He thinks he is smarter than I am," "She never does her share of the work around here," "She will never change because she just wants to take advantage of me," or "He wants me to do everything his way").

15. Teach the student realistic, positive self-talk to increase his/her sense of peace and fairness in negotiating conflicts (e.g., "I am a reasonable and intelligent person," "We can talk about a reasonable way to share chores," or "She will want to work out our differences as much as I want to").

7. Identify and replace irrational beliefs that block effective communication and conflict resolution. (16, 17)

16. Assist the student in identifying his/her irrational beliefs that act as barriers to effective conflict resolution (e.g., "Everyone wants to take advantage of me," "My roommate is the cause of all our problems," or "I cannot tolerate someone who is so different than me").

17. Teach the student to rationally reframe his/her irrational beliefs to remove barriers to conflict resolution (e.g., "Most people are kind and considerate of others," "I have to believe that I contribute to our problems in some way," or "Learning to re-spect and appreciate differences in people is constructive and mature").

8. Implement relaxation tech-niques during conflict resolu-tion with roommates. (18, 19)

18. Teach the student deep muscle, deep breathing and positive imagery relaxation techniques to better manage stress and anxiety

caused by interpersonal difficulties.

19. Assign the student the task of implementing positive self-talk, reframed beliefs and relaxation techniques in daily conflict management with roommates or community living members; process the results, reinforcing success and redirecting failure.

9. Identify a support system in the residence-hall environment that will encourage and assist with the roommate conflict resolution. (20, 21)

20. Explore peer resources available to the student in mediating or offering suggestions for conflict resolution between the student and his/her roommate.

21. Explore administrative staff support (e.g., resident advisor, residence director) available to provide the student with suggestions or mediation of his/her conflict with the roommate.

10. Monitor roommate interactions to identify ways to improve communication and reduce conflict. (22, 23)

22. Assign the student a daily journal to track his/her interactions with others in the residence community; process the journal material to gain insight into the nature of the student's relationships and conflict resolution style.

23. Review the student's roommate interaction journal then ask him/her to list three ways he/she could improve his/her communication and conflict resolution behaviors.

11. Report success in implementing assertive communication. (24, 25, 26)

24. Refer the student to an assertiveness training group or teach him/her assertive communication techniques and their advantage over aggressive, passive-aggressive, or passive

patterns of reaction to interpersonal problems.

25. Use role-play and modeling to teach the student the application of assertiveness to his/her roommate conflict situations; encourage his/her implementation of assertiveness on a daily basis.

26. Review the student's experience with assertiveness, reinforcing success and redirecting failure.

12. Verbalize an increased awareness of the need for personal boundaries and when they are violated. (27, 28, 29, 30)

27. Assist the student in developing new boundaries for not accepting responsibility for other's actions or feelings.

28. Ask the student to journal daily about boundaries for taking responsibility for self and others and when he/she is aware of boundaries being ignored by self or others.

29. Assign the student reading on setting personal boundaries (e.g., *Boundaries: Where You End and I Begin* by Katherine or *A Gift to Myself* by Whitfield); process the student's understanding of key ideas.

30. Review the student's attempts to set personal boundaries; reinforce his/her success and redirect failure.

13. Increase involvement in structured social activities available on campus and decrease involvement with roommates. (31, 32, 33)

31. Assist the student in completing a concentric circle diagram of his/her social relationships; evaluate the diagram for the depth and breath of the student's social network outside of his/her roommates.

32. Encourage the student to broaden his/her social network

and to decrease reliance on his/her roommates for socialization and recreation.

33. Explore areas of campus life that could bring increased socialization and distraction from roommate issues (e.g., campus clubs and organizations, part-time employment, intramural sports, or religious activities and groups) with the student.

14. Implement new social skills by reaching out to establish new social relationships. (34, 35, 36, 37, 38)

34. Teach the student the acronym SOFTEN, which represents the elements of social readiness (**S**miling, **O**pen posture, **F**orward leaning, **T**ouch, **E**ye contact, **N**odding); encourage him/her to apply these behaviors to initiating social contact.

35. Ask the student to commit to trying SOFTEN and one new social behavior during the week (e.g., initiating a conversation, sustaining a conversation, or inviting someone for coffee); process the results, reinforcing success and redirecting failure.

36. Teach the student active listening skills including (a) listening with full attention, (b) listening for the feelings as well as threw content, and (c) paraphrasing to show that the message has been heard.

37. Teach the student the concept and advantage of I statements ("I feel _____ when you _____ because _____; I would like it if you _____").

38. Encourage the student's use of active listening skills and I statements during the week; process the results, reinforcing success and redirecting failure.

—. _____   —. _____
   _____   _____

—. _____   —. _____
   _____   _____

—. _____   —. _____
   _____   _____

DIAGNOSTIC SUGGESTIONS:

Axis I: 309.0   Adjustment Disorder with Depressed Mood
                309.3   Adjustment Disorder with Disturbance of
                           Conduct
                309.24   Adjustment Disorder with Anxiety
                309.28   Adjustment Disorder with Mixed Anxiety and
                           Depressed Mood
                300.23   Social Phobia
                300.02   Generalized Anxiety Disorder
                300.4   Dysthymic Disorder

                _____   _____

                _____   _____

Axis II: 301.20   Schizoid Personality Disorder
                301.6   Dependent Personality Disorder

                _____   _____

                _____   _____

SELF-ESTEEM DEFICIT

BEHAVIORAL DEFINITIONS

1. Rejects or discounts compliments offered by others toward self.
2. Frequently makes self-disparaging remarks about academic ability, appearance, social life, and/or other aspects of self.
3. Sees self as unattractive, worthless, a loser, and/or unimportant when comparing self to classmates and/or others.
4. Takes blame easily and readily, whether or not at fault.
5. Lacks pride in grooming.
6. Has difficulty saying, "No" to others' requests for personal favors.
7. Assumes not being liked by others.
8. Fears rejection from others, especially by roommates, classmates, and/or other members of peer group.
9. Lacks defined goals for the college experience and setting of inappropriately low goals for academic performance.
10. Is unable to identify and verbalize positive aspects about self.
11. Is uncomfortable in social situations, especially in larger groups, class discussion, and group activities.

___. _____
_____

___. _____
_____

___. _____
_____

LONG-TERM GOALS

1. Elevate self-esteem.
2. Develop a consistently positive self-image.
3. Demonstrate improved self-esteem through more pride in appearance, more assertiveness, greater eye contact during conversations, and identification of positive traits in self-talk.
4. Experience less anxiety in social, group, and classroom situations and interactions.
5. Demonstrate greater confidence in self and in academic abilities.
6. Establish appropriately elevated goals for college experience and life following graduation.
7. Demonstrate improved skills in initiating appropriate social contacts in various academic and nonacademic situations.

—. _____
   _____
   _____

—. _____
   _____
   _____

—. _____
   _____

SHORT-TERM OBJECTIVES

1. Describe the nature and history of feelings of low self-esteem. (1, 2, 3)

THERAPEUTIC INTERVENTIONS

1. Actively built a level of trust with the student using consistent eye contact, active listening, unconditional positive regard, and warm acceptance to increase his/her ability to identify and express feelings of low self-esteem.

2. Assist the student in identifying and clarifying feelings of low self-esteem in the college setting.

3. Explore the student's history of feelings of low self-esteem from the past through the present.

2. Identify the historical and current sources of low self-esteem. (4, 5)

3. Identify any secondary gain that is received by speaking negatively about self and/or refusing to experiment with alternative behaviors. (6, 7)

4. Decrease the frequency of negative, disparaging self-talk and increase the frequency of positive self-descriptive statements. (8, 9, 10, 11)

4. Help the student clarify the current causes of his/her feelings of low self-esteem (e.g., social rejection or academic struggles).

5. Explore the student's family and childhood history for causes of low self-esteem (e.g., abuse, neglect, abandonment, or severe criticism).

6. Teach the student the meaning and power of secondary gain in maintaining negative behavior patterns.

7. Assist the student in identifying how self-disparagement and avoidance of new behaviors could bring secondary gain (e.g., praise from others or others taking over responsibilities).

8. Assist the student in identifying his/her negative, distorted self-talk that precipitates or mediates feelings of experience of low self-esteem, anxiety, distrust, or defensiveness (e.g., "I'm a nobody here," "She would never want to go out with me," or "I'll never make the team).

9. Teach the student realistic, positive self-talk to increase his/her sense of reality and fairness (e.g., "I am new here, but I can learn to make new friends"; "Perhaps it is worth the risk to ask her to coffee"; or "If I focus my training, I do stand a good chance of getting on the team").

10. Gently confront, challenge, and/or reframe the student's self-disparaging remarks.

5. Increase the frequency of assertive and problem-solving behaviors with roommates, other residents in the dormitory, classmates, and/or faculty. (12, 13, 14, 15)

11. Assign the student self-esteem building exercises (e.g., see *The Building Blocks of Self-Esteem* by Shapiro, *Ten Days to Self-Esteem* by Burns, or *What to Say When You Talk to Yourself* by Helmstetter); process the results.

12. Introduce the student to a model for assertive dialog that respectfully identifies issues in behavioral terms, recognizes both individuals' needs and rights, and offers possible solutions that are mutually beneficial.

13. Teach the student effective conflict-resolution or problem-solving skills: (a) problem identification or clarification in behavioral terms; (b) mutual brainstorming of possible alternative solutions and review of the pros and cons of each; (c) mutual selection of an alternative solution for implementation; (d) evaluation of the outcome in terms of mutual satisfaction; and (e) adjustment of the solution, if necessary, to increase mutual satisfaction.

14. Use role-play and modeling to teach the application of eye contact, assertiveness, and problem solving to the student's current experience of low self-esteem.

15. Review the student's progress in asserting himself/herself in social situations; reinforce success and redirect failure.

6. Identify and replace irrational beliefs that act to support feelings of low self-esteem. (11, 16, 17)

11. Assign the student self-esteem building exercises (e.g., see *The Building Blocks of Self-Esteem* by Shapiro, *Ten Days to*

Self-Esteem by Burns, or *What to Say When You Talk to Yourself* by Helmstetter); process the results.

16. Assist the student in identifying his/her irrational beliefs that act as barriers to effective coping (e.g., "I'm such a loser, no one would want to get to know me"; "I'm so pathetic and uninteresting that I'll have no social life here"; or "I'm so dumb, I'll likely flunk out this semester").

17. Teach the student to rationally reframe his/her irrational beliefs to remove barriers to more positive self-esteem (e.g., "Most people here are also new, so they are likely experiencing the same feelings as me"; "I bet I can find some campus clubs related to my interests and hobbies"; or "Classes are tougher than in high school, but I can get a tutor if I need").

7. Implement behavioral changes to counteract feelings of low self-esteem and build confidence. (18, 19)

18. Assist the student in identifying and listing his/her typical avoidant behavioral responses to the experience of low self-esteem.

19. Assist the student in listing his/her positive traits and accomplishments; integrating this list into his/her self-image.

8. Identify and verbalize daily positive personal traits and accomplishments. (20, 21, 22)

20. Assist the student in developing a behavioral coping plan for each fear that is associated with low self-esteem (e.g., implementing assertiveness, problem solving, or social skills; initiating social contact to build a network; making contact with groups of students with similar

interests; or utilizing tutor services on campus).

21. Ask the student to make at least one positive statement about himself/herself daily and record it in a journal and process the experience in session.

22. Assign mirror exercises of the student talking positively about himself/herself.

9. Identify a support system in the residence hall environment that will encourage and assist with periods in which feelings of low self-esteem manifest. (23, 24)

23. Explore the peer resources (e.g., planned group activities, socials, study groups, or parties) available to the student in mediating or offering suggestions for support and getting involved in social activities.

24. Explore administrative staff support (e.g., resident advisor or residence director) available to provide him/her with suggestions for available options to help to build confidence and social opportunities.

10. Identify experiences of rejection of abuse and their impact on current feelings about self and others. (25, 26)

25. Help the student become aware of his/her current fear of rejection and its connection with past rejection of abandonment experiences.

26. Explore and interpret the student's incidents of abuse (e.g., emotional, physical, and/or sexual) and how they have impacted current feelings about himself/herself and unmet needs for nurture and approval.

11. Form realistic, appropriate, and attainable goals for the college experience, academic performance, and socially. (27, 28)

27. Assist the student in evaluating his/her goals to ensure that they are realistic and attainable.

28. Assign the student homework of making a list of goals for

various areas of campus life, academic performance, social experiences, and develop a plan for steps toward goal attainment.

12. List unmet needs for self-fulfillment. (25, 26, 29)

25. Help the student become aware of his/her current fear of rejection and its connection with past rejection of abandonment experiences.

26. Explore and interpret the student's incidents of abuse (e.g., emotional, physical, and/ or sexual) and how they have impacted current feelings about himself/herself and unmet needs for nurture and approval.

29. Use role-play and role reversal techniques to assist the student in becoming capable of identifying and verbalizing his/her needs.

13. Articulate a plan to be proactive to get identified needs met. (30, 31)

30. Conduct a conjoint or family therapy session in which the student is supported in appropriately expressing his/her unmet needs and developing a plan for need satisfaction.

31. Assist the student in developing a specific action plan to get needs met appropriately with friends, roommates, and faculty.

14. Increase eye contact with others in the classroom, dormitory, and other social situations. (14, 32, 33)

14. Use role-play and modeling to teach the application of eye contact, assertiveness, and problem solving to the student's current experience of low self-esteem.

32. Gently confront the student when he/she is observed avoiding eye contact.

33. Assign the student the task of making eye contact with whom-ever he/she is speaking.

15. Take responsibility for devel-oping and maintaining daily grooming and personal hygiene routine. (34)

34. Monitor and give feedback to the student on his/her grooming and hygiene.

16. Positively acknowledge verbal compliments from others without discounting. (35)

35. Ask the student to be aware of, record, and acknowledge graciously (without discounting) praising compliments from others; practice in session via role play and role reversal.

__. _____

_____

__. _____

_____

__. _____

_____

__. _____

_____

__. _____

_____

__. _____

_____

DIAGNOSTIC SUGGESTIONS:

Axis I:	300.4	Dysthymic Disorder
	300.23	Social Phobia
	296.xx	Major Depressive Disorder
	309.0	Adjustment Disorder with Depressed Mood
	296.xx	Bipolar I Disorder
	296.89	Bipolar II Disorder
	_____	_____
	_____	_____
Axis II:	301.83	Borderline Personality Disorder
	799.9	Diagnosis Deferred
	V71.09	No Diagnosis
	_____	_____
	_____	_____

SELF-MUTILATION/BORDERLINE PERSONALITY

BEHAVIORAL DEFINITIONS

1. Extremely emotionally reactive under minor stress that usually results in the uncontrollable impulse to superficially harm oneself.
2. Demonstrates a pattern of intense, chaotic interpersonal relationships with roommates, classmates, friends, family, and/or faculty.
3. Exhibits marked identity disturbance.
4. Engages in impulsive behaviors that are potentially physically self-damaging.
5. Engages in recurrent suicidal gestures, threats, or self-mutilating behavior.
6. Has a positive history of suicide attempts that required professional or family/friend intervention on some level (e.g., inpatient hospitalization, outpatient care, emergency medical intervention, or close supervision by concerned others).
7. Chronically feels empty, bored, alienated, dependent, and/or isolated.
8. Frequently erupts with intense, inappropriate anger.
9. Easily feels that roommates, classmates, friends, family, and/or faculty are treating him/her unfairly or that they can't be trusted.

___. _____

_____

___. _____

_____

___. _____

_____

LONG-TERM GOALS

1. Eliminate superficial, self-damaging behaviors.
2. Develop and demonstrate coping skills to deal with extremes of mood and reduce impulsive behavior.
3. Alleviate suicidal impulses/ideation and return to a sense of hope for self, life, academic, and social activities as well as the future.
4. Develop the ability to control impulses, curb acting-out behaviors, and conduct self properly on campus and with others.
5. Develop and demonstrate anger management skills.
6. Learn and practice interpersonal relationship skills that are based in trust of others.
7. Share emotions with family, roommates, friends, counselors, and/or others in an appropriate manner.

__. _____
   _____
   _____
__. _____
   _____
   _____
__. _____
   _____

SHORT-TERM OBJECTIVES

1. Verbalize the intense feelings that motivate self-mutilating behaviors and how those feelings are relieved by such behaviors. (1, 2)

2. Describe the history and nature of self-mutilating behaviors

THERAPEUTIC INTERVENTIONS

1. Actively build a level of trust with the student using consistent eye contact, active listening, unconditional positive regard, and warm acceptance to increase his/her ability to identify and express thoughts and feelings related to impulsive, self-harming behaviors.

2. Assist the student in identifying and clarifying specific feelings and problems that lead to the urge to engage in self-harm in the college setting.

3. Explore the student's history of self-harm behavior from

before coming to college and since. (3)

3. Verbalize a promise to contact supportive and caring others if a serious urge of self-harm arises. (4, 5)

the past through to the present.

4. Obtain a promise from the student that he/she will initiate contact with the counselor, a hospital emergency room, or crisis help line if the suicidal urge become strong and before any self-injurious behaviors occur; provide him/her with a 24-hour emergency crisis help telephone number.

5. Share the contract of preventative action with his/her roommate, family, and/or significant others after obtaining appropriate written consent from the student.

4. Cooperate with hospitalization if the self-harming urge becomes suicidal, uncontrollable, or markedly severe. (6)

6. Arrange for hospitalization if the student is judged be at risk for uncontrollable harm to himself/herself.

5. Cooperate with an evaluation to determine the necessity for medication. (7)

7. Refer the student to a psychiatrist to evaluate the depth of his/her depression, level of lethality, suicidal potential, and need for psychopharmacological intervention.

6. Take medication as ordered and report the side effects as well as the efficacy of the medication. (8)

8. Monitor the student for the therapeutic effect and/or side-effects as well as compliance with the prescribed psychotropic medication; confer with the prescribing physician on a regular basis with the student's consent.

7. Complete a psychological evaluation to assess current emotional and cognitive functioning and aid in differential diagnosis. (9)

9. Conduct or arrange for a psychological assessment of the student's mental and emotional status; report results (after obtaining appropriate consent) to family, consulting physician,

8. Write a daily journal noting self-defeating thoughts, feelings, and resultant behaviors. (10, 11)

9. Identify and replace irrational beliefs and/or negative self-talk that block effective problem-solving and/or emotional expression that may lead to feelings of self-harm and substitute with more realistic, accurate, and positive thoughts and messages to mitigate the urge to self-harm. (12, 13)

10. Identify and replace distorted cognitive interpretations of circumstances and events that

and/or the student, as appropriate.

10. Request that the student keep a daily journal noting feelings, mood, situations, and resultant behaviors; process his/her experiences of reasons for, reasons against, consequences of, and feelings about self-mutilation.

11. Request that the student keep a daily record of self-defeating thoughts (e.g., hopelessness, helplessness, worthlessness, catastrophizing, or negatively predicting the future), and challenge each thought for accuracy; replace each dysfunctional thought with one that is realistic, positive, and self-enhancing.

12. Assist the student in identifying his/her irrational beliefs that act as barriers to effectively coping with feelings of suicidal ideation and/or feelings of self-harm (e.g., "It's better to deal physically with my emotional pain").

13. Teach the student to rationally reframe his/her irrational beliefs to remove barriers to feelings of suicidal ideation and/or self-harm (e.g., "I do get upset, but there are also times when I can manage stresses quite well" or "There are some people here at college who really do seem to care about me").

14. Assist the student in identifying his/her negative, distorted self-talk that precipitates or mediates

trigger the impulse to self-harm. (14, 15)

the impulse of self-harm (e.g., "No one really cares about me," "They have no idea how much pain I'm in," or "Things will never get better").

15. Teach realistic, positive self-talk to increase a sense of the positive aspects of his/her life (e.g., "I am an intelligent person that has had some problems, but I am quite capable of learning new ways to deal with my problems more effectively" or "At times it may seem that things will never improve, but with help, support, and working at it, they will").

11. Compile a list of negative consequences to self and others resulting from self-harming behaviors. (16)

16. Assign the student to list the destructive consequences to himself/herself and others resulting from his/her self-mutilating behaviors.

12. Implement behavioral coping strategies to exercise greater self-control to overcome the impulse to self-mutilate. (17, 18, 19)

17. Assist the student in developing a behavioral coping plan for self-mutilating impulses (e.g., learning assertiveness, stress management, or social skills; holding an ice cube; vigorous physical activities, such as sprints, running in place, push-ups, or squeezing a tennis ball).

18. Assist the student in developing coping strategies for dealing with self-harming triggers (e.g., more physical exercise, discuss with a roommate or counselor, greater engagement in academic work/ classes, less internal focus, increased social involvement, reliance on faith, engagement in extracurricular activities, or more frequent expression of feelings in an appropriate manor).

19. Teach the student effective problem-solving skills: (a) problem identification or clarification in behavioral terms; (b) mutual brainstorming of possible alternative solutions and review of the pros and cons of each; (c) mutual selection of an alternative solution for implementation; (d) evaluation of the outcome in terms of mutual satisfaction; and (e) adjustment of the solution, if necessary, to increase mutual satisfaction.

13. Implement cognitive coping strategies to exercise greater self-control to overcome the impulse to self-mutilate. (20, 21)

20. Teach the student cognitive methods (e.g., thought stoppage, thought substitution, or reframing) for gaining and improving control over impulsive, self-mutilating behaviors.

21. Identify and confront catastrophizing tendencies in the student's cognitive processing, allowing for a more realistic perspective of hope in the face of painful situations and train him/her to revise core schemes using cognitive restructuring techniques (e.g., countering all-or-none thinking, or catastrophizing).

14. Describe specific situations in which the strategy of stop, look, listen, and think was implemented on campus, in class, and/or elsewhere. (22, 23)

22. Teach the student the mediational and self-control strategies of stop, look, listen, and think to inhibit his/her impulsivity and diminish self-mutilating behavior.

23. Use role-play and modeling to apply the strategy of stop, look, listen, and think to the student's daily life experiences; urge implementation of this

technique and process the results.

15. Practice relaxation training to reduce muscle tension and facilitate sleep. (24, 25)

24. Teach the student relaxation methods (e.g., progressive muscle relaxation or guided, visual imagery) to better deal with stressful situations.

25. Monitor the student's sleep patterns and educate him/her on biofeedback, self-hypnosis, and other methods of body control to facilitate restorative, restful sleep.

16. Learn and apply assertiveness skills as a means of mitigating impulsive acting out and better, more adaptive problem-solving. (26, 27)

26. Use modeling and role-playing to instruct the student in methods of assertive interaction with others or refer him/her to an assertiveness training class or group.

27. Encourage the student to implement healthy assertiveness in his/her daily life; monitor, reinforcing success and redirecting failure.

17. Participate in family therapy sessions to identify feelings and resolve conflicts related to family members and self-mutilating behaviors. (28, 29, 30)

28. Probe the student's feelings of despair related to his/her family relationships.

29. Meet with the student's significant others, roommates, family, and/or friends, to assess their understanding of the causes of the student's distress.

30. Conduct family therapy sessions to identify familial factors contributing to self-mutilation.

18. Participate in family therapy so they will learn ways to better respond and support the diminution of self-mutilating behaviors. (31, 32, 33)

31. Educate the family about self-mutilation and methods of offering emotional support to the student.

32. Conduct family therapy sessions to promote communication of

the student's feelings of sadness, hurt, and/or anger.

33. Instruct (after obtaining appropriate consents) family members to be sensitive to the reoccurrence of suicidal ideation or self-mutilation in the student (e.g., an attempt, preoccupation with death, or significant social withdrawal); provide methods of therapeutic response (e.g., contacting the counselor and/or emergency services).

19. Identify a support system in the residence-hall environment that will encourage and assist during times experiencing feelings of self-harm. (34)

34. Explore administrative staff support (e.g., resident advisor or residence director) available to provide the student with help if feelings of suicidal ideation and/or feelings of self-harm become difficult to manage.

20. Verbalize an absence of self-harming incidents. (10, 15, 18, 20, 35)

10. Request that the student keep a daily journal noting feelings, mood, situations, and resultant behaviors; process his/her experiences of the reasons for, reasons against, consequences of, and feelings about self-mutilation.

15. Teach realistic, positive self-talk to increase a sense of the positive aspects of his/her life (e.g., "I am an intelligent person that has had some problems, but I am quite capable of learning new ways to deal with my problems more effectively" or "At times it may seem that things will never improve, but with help, support, and working at it, they will").

18. Assist the student in developing coping strategies for dealing with self-harming triggers (e.g., more physical exercise, discuss with a roommate or counselor, greater engagement in academic work/classes, less internal focus, increased social involvement, reliance on faith, engagement in extracurricular activities, or more frequent expression of feelings in an appropriate manor).

20. Teach the student cognitive methods (e.g., thought stoppage, thought substitution, or reframing) for gaining and improving control over impulsive, self-mutilating behaviors.

35. Monitor the student's urges for suicide or self-mutilation; arrange for more structured, intense treatment if necessary and reinforce successful progress as appropriate.

—. _____   —. _____
    _____   _____

—. _____   —. _____
    _____   _____

—. _____   —. _____
    _____   _____

DIAGNOSTIC SUGGESTIONS:

Axis I:

300.4	Dysthymic Disorder
296.xx	Bipolar I Disorder
296.2x	Major Depressive Disorder, Single Episode
296.3x	Major Depressive Disorder, Recurrent
296.89	Bipolar II Disorder
312.30	Impulse Control Disorder

_____   _____

_____   _____

Axis II:

301.83	Borderline Personality Disorder
799.9	Diagnosis Deferred
V71.09	No Diagnosis

_____   _____

_____   _____

SEXUAL ACTIVITY CONCERNS

BEHAVIORAL DEFINITIONS

1. Has engaged in sexual activity with several different partners with little or no emotional attachment.
2. Engages in sexual intercourse without birth control and without interest in and/or ability to take responsibility for a child.
3. Is sexually active with one partner with no sense of commitment to each other.
4. Does not utilize safe-sex practices.
5. Uses drugs and/or alcohol to alter mood and judgment prior to and during sexual activity.
6. Equates sexual relationship with genuine and meaningful intimacy.
7. Uses sex to enhance mood and feelings of self-worth.
8. Consents to involvement in sexual activity that is diminishing and degrading.
9. Avoids and/or is repulsed by any and all sexual contact, even in the context of a long-term, mutually caring relationship.
10. Consistently lacks physiological response and/or subjective sense of pleasure during sexual activity.
11. Family of origin's stance on sexuality is rigid, hypocritical, and/or without boundaries.

Some material in this chapter was adapted from *The Adolescent Psychotherapy Treatment Planner* by A. E. Jongsma, L. M. Peterson, and W. P. McInnis (New York: John Wiley & Sons, 2003). © 2003 by Arthur E. Jongsma, Jr., L. Mark Peterson, and William P. McInnis. Reprinted with permission.

—. _____

—. _____

—. _____

LONG-TERM GOALS

1. Understand the components of a healthy relationship.
2. Engage in sexual activity only in the context of a relationship that is committed, emotionally intimate, caring, and respectful.
3. Always practice birth control and safe sex.
4. Terminate substance use, recognizing the link between use of alcohol/drugs and poor sexual choices and/or violent sexual behavior.
5. Increase desire for and/or enjoyment of sexual activity.
6. Resolve family-of-origin conflicts that result in maladaptive sexual behaviors.

—. _____

—. _____

—. _____

SHORT-TERM OBJECTIVES

1. Acknowledge sexual history and current sexual practices. (1, 2)

THERAPEUTIC INTERVENTIONS

1. Gather a detailed sexual history from the student that includes the number of sexual partners, frequency of sexual activity, birth control, safe-sex practices used, degree of attachment to partner(s), source of sexual information in childhood, and initial sexual experiences.

2. Provide information about family-of-origin experiences that have influenced sexual attitudes, feelings, and behavior. (3, 4)

2. Explore the student's thoughts and feelings surrounding the facts of his/her sexual history and current activities.

3. Examine the role of the student's religious training in reinforcing feelings of rebellion, guilt, and/or shame about sexual thoughts and behaviors.

4. Investigate the role of the student's family in instilling negative attitudes and/or a promiscuous approach toward sexual activity.

3. Disclose any history of sexual abuse and its effect on current sexual activity. (5, 6)

5. Support the student in revealing any history of sexual abuse (see Childhood Abuse chapter in this *Planner*).

6. Assist the student in making connections between the experiences of sexual abuse in childhood and his/her current sexual practices (e.g., hooking up with a new person every time he/she goes out, refusing to participate in any relationship that could have a sexual component, involvement in sexually violent/dangerous behaviors because he/she is already damaged goods).

4. Verbalize an understanding of the role of childhood experiences in the development of unhealthy sexual attitudes and responses. (6, 7)

6. Assist the student in making connections between the experience of sexual abuse in childhood and his/her current sexual practices (e.g., hooking up with a new person every time he/she goes out, refusing to participate in any relationship that could have a sexual component, involvement in sexually violent/dangerous

behaviors because he/she is already damaged goods).

7. Help the student gain insight into the impact of unhealthy/abusive sexual attitudes, messages, and experiences of childhood on the development of maladaptive sexual practices or sexual dysfunction.

5. Verbalize insight into the sources and impact of low self-esteem. (8, 9, 10)

8. Explore the student's feelings about himself/herself and the ways in which he/she expresses and acts on them (see Self-Esteem Deficit chapter in this *Planner*).

9. Assist the student in identifying sources of his/her self-esteem deficits (e.g., academic failures; poor body image; destructive peer interactions; abusive, critical, and/or rejecting parents).

10. Help the student connect his/her responses to sexual activities to his/her negative sense and treatment of himself/herself.

6. Identify positive ways to build self-esteem. (11, 12, 13, 14)

11. Encourage the student to replace sexual activities with nurturing activities that would enhance his/her self-esteem (e.g., making a favorite comfort food, watching a favorite video with friends, or volunteering for an organization with a mission that is important to him/her).

12. Refer the student to a campus therapy or support group.

13. Suggest that the student become involved in yoga, a self-defense class, weight and strength training, or some other form of physical activity that can provide a sense of accomplishment

as well as a positive connection with his/her body.

14. Ask the student to create several affirmations, prominently post them in his/her room, and read them aloud several times a day.

7. Identify the characteristics of a healthy relationship, including emotional intimacy, commitment, and passion. (15)

15. Using Sternberg's model of love, help the student understand the distinctions between intimacy, passion, and commitment (e.g., Intimacy = Closeness, affection, connectedness; Passion = Sex drive, physical closeness, romance; Decision/commitment = Decision to or recognition of love followed by the commitment to maintain love); discuss his/her ability to make these distinctions in his/her current relationships (see Intimacy/Commitment Issues chapter in this *Planner*).

8. Verbalize the risks involved in forgetting or refusing to use birth control or safe-sex practices and commit to observing these practices in all future sexual encounters. (16, 17, 18)

16. Refer the student to the student health center, Planned Parenthood, or community clinic to be tested for sexually transmitted diseases and/or pregnancy and to receive treatment and medical care as appropriate.

17. Explore magical thinking or underlying concerns that have influenced the student's behavior about use of birth control and safe-sex practices (e.g., getting pregnant is impossible since it hasn't happened yet; condoms take all the fun out of sex; birth control is the woman's problem; someone that nice would never have a sexually transmitted disease); assist the student in

refuting these cognitive distortions.

18. Follow up to ensure that the student has obtained the necessary medical prescriptions and/or over-the-counter remedies to practice birth control and safe sex.

9. Abstain from using drugs and/or alcohol as vehicles to allow or interfere with sexual responsiveness. (19, 20, 21)

19. Examine the student's reasons for using drugs/alcohol as a prelude to or in conjunction with sexual activity.

20. Assist the student in recognizing that drugs/alcohol serve to quiet inhibitions as well as feelings of guilt and shame associated with sexual activity.

21. Refer the student to AA, NA, OA or ACOA groups on campus (see Chemical Dependence/ Abuse chapter in this *Planner*).

10. Verbalize healthy acceptance and accurate knowledge of human sexuality. (22, 23, 24)

22. Ask the student to use appropriate language for sexual body parts, feelings, and behaviors; use modeling and reinforcement to encourage this behavior.

23. Assign reading that provides accurate information on sexuality (*The College Student's Health Guide* by Smith and Smith), sexually transmitted diseases (www.plannedparenthood.org), and the impact of biography on biology (*Anatomy of the Spirit* by Myss).

24. Process human sexuality information with the student and reinforce his/her ability to discuss sexuality knowledgeably and positively.

11. Demonstrate selective, appropriate, and healthy sexual behaviors. (25, 26, 27)

25. Support the student in building emotional intimacy and commitment with a specific partner before becoming sexually involved.

26. Reinforce the student's abstinence from using alcohol and/or drugs in conjunction with sexual activity.

27. Meet weekly during the semester to discuss any concerns that might arise about the student's ability to maintain strong, positive relationships, and healthy sexual practices.

__. _____   __. _____
     _____   _____
__. _____   __. _____
     _____   _____
__. _____   __. _____
     _____   _____

DIAGNOSTIC SUGGESTIONS:

Axis I:	300.4	Dysthymic Disorder
	305.00	Alcohol Abuse
	308.3	Acute Stress Disorder
	296.xx	Bipolar I Disorder
	296.89	Bipolar II Disorder
	301.13	Cyclothymic Disorder
	313.82	Identity Problem
	304.89	Polysubstance Dependence
	V62.89	Phase of Life Problem
	V71.09	No Diagnosis
	799.9	Diagnosis Deferred

_____ _____

_____ _____

Axis II: 301.50   Histrionic Personality Disorder
               301.9   Personality Disorder NOS
               V71.09   No Diagnosis
               799.9   Diagnosis Deferred

               _____   _____

               _____   _____

SEXUAL IDENTITY ISSUES

BEHAVIORAL DEFINITIONS

1. Feels uncertain about personal sexual orientation.
2. Lacks arousal or desire for opposite-sex partner.
3. Has sexual fantasies and desires about same-sex people, which cause emotional distress.
4. Enjoys sexual activity with someone of the same sex, which causes confusion, guilt, and/or anxiety.
5. Verbalizes depressed mood and diminished interest in campus and academic activities.
6. Experiences intimate relationship conflicts caused by uncertainty about sexual orientation.
7. Verbalizes feelings of guilt, shame, and/or worthlessness based on sexual identity confusion.
8. Conceals sexual identity from significant others (e.g., friends, roommate, and/or family).
9. Has concerns about negative reactions from others on campus if sexual identity is made public.

—. _____

_____

—. _____

_____

—. _____

_____

Some material in this chapter was adapted from the Sexual Identity Confusion—Adult chapter in *The Gay and Lesbian Psychotherapy Treatment Planner* by J. M. Evosevich and Michael Avriette (New York: John Wiley & Sons, 2000). © 2000 by J. M. Evosevich and Michael Avriette. Reprinted with permission.

LONG-TERM GOALS

1. Identify sexual identity and engage in pursuing a wide range of relationship interests.
2. Reduce overall intensity of the anxiety associated with sexual identity so that daily functioning and academic performance is not impaired.
3. Disclose sexual orientation to significant others.
4. Return to previous levels of emotional, psychological, and social functioning.
5. Eliminate all signs of depression (e.g., sad mood, guilt, withdrawal, or worthlessness).

—. _____
   _____
—. _____
   _____
—. _____
   _____

SHORT-TERM OBJECTIVES

1. Discuss the difficulties experienced with being in college and having mixed emotions concerning sexuality and orientation. (1, 2, 3)

THERAPEUTIC INTERVENTIONS

1. Actively build a level of trust with the student with consistent eye contact, active listening, unconditional positive regard, and warm acceptance of the student to increase his/her ability to identify and express feelings of fear, anxiety, and distress over sexual identity confusion.

2. Assist the student in identifying and clarifying specific feelings and problems that spring from fear, anxiety, and distress over sexual identity confusion in the college setting.

3. Assess opportunities the student has taken advantage of or avoided to become less

troubled by fear, anxiety, and distress over sexual identity confusion in the college environment.

2. Openly discuss the history of sexual desires, fantasies, and/or experiences. (4, 5)

4. Explore the student's history of sexual activity, fantasies, and thoughts beginning with childhood through adolescence to current.

5. Assist the student in identifying sexual experiences throughout his/her life that have been a source of excitement, satisfaction, and/or emotional gratification.

3. Keep a journal describing sexual thoughts, fantasies, and/or conflicts that occur throughout the week. (6, 7)

6. Assign the student a journal to describe sexual thoughts, fantasies, and/or conflicts that occur throughout the week, assisting him/her by increasing awareness of sexual attractions and conflicts.

7. Assign the student the task of rating sexual attraction to men and women on a scale of 1 to 10 (with 10 being extremely attractive and 1 being not at all attractive); ask him/her to record these ratings in a journal on a daily basis as he/she interacts with others.

4. Verbalize an understanding about how religious, cultural, racial, and/or ethnic identity contributes to confusion about sexual identity. (8, 9)

8. Explore how the student's cultural, ethnic, and/or racial group defines and views homosexual and/or bisexual behavior and/or identity.

9. Explore the student's religious convictions and how these may conflict with identifying himself/herself as homosexual or bisexual and cause feelings of shame or guilt.

5. Discuss concerns about sexual orientation in the college setting. (10, 11)

6. Verbalize an understanding of the range of sexual identities. (12, 13, 14)

7. Identify the negative emotions experienced by hiding or denying sexuality. (15, 16)

10. Review any concerns about coming out in relation to potential conflicts that may occur with roommates, team mates, or classmates involved in extracurricular activities.

11. Explore for any interpersonal conflicts the student has experienced because of his/her sexual identity exploration (e.g., teasing, rejection, shunning, or avoidance of the subject).

12. Discuss various aspects of the varieties of human sexuality, (e.g., heterosexual, homosexual, bisexual, and transgendered).

13. Assign the student homework of writing three biographies describing his/her life 20 years in the future—one as a heterosexual, one as a homosexual, and/or one as a bisexual; process the content in a subsequent session (e.g., ask him/her which life was more satisfying or had more regrets).

14. Ask the student to read *The Invention of Heterosexuality* by Katz; process the content in subsequent sessions.

15. Explore the negative emotions related to the student hiding/denying his/her sexuality (e.g., shame, guilt, anxiety, or loneliness).

16. Explore whether the student has had suicidal thoughts related to his/her sexual identity; take precautions to protect him/her from harming himself/herself by arranging for psychiatric

hospitalization and/or structured 24-hour supervision by significant others (see Suicidal Ideation chapter in this *Planner*).

8. Verbalize an understanding of safe-sex practices and implement these practices. (17, 18)

17. Teach the details of safe-sex guidelines and encourage the student to include them in all future sexual activities.

18. Monitor the student's use of safe-sex practices, reinforcing for success and redirecting failure.

9. List 10 myths about homosexuals, bisexuals, and heterosexuals and discuss more realistic perspectives. (19)

19. Assign the student homework of identifying 10 myths about homosexuals or bisexuals and assist in replacing them with more realistic, positive perspectives.

10. Discuss concerns about sexual orientation in the context of how his/her family will react to it. (20, 21)

20. Discuss how the student expects his/her family members to react when learning of his/her sexual orientation and plan ways for him/her to respond.

21. Assign the student homework of writing a description of telling his/her family of his/her sexual identity, detailing how each member might react to the revelation.

11. List the advantages and disadvantages of disclosing sexual orientation to significant people in his/her life. (22, 23, 24)

22. Assign the student homework of listing the advantages and disadvantages of disclosing sexual orientation to significant others (e.g., family, roommates, classmates, teammates, friends); process the list in subsequent sessions.

23. Use role-play and role-reversal to disclose the student's sexual orientation to significant others; process the feelings generated by this exercise.

24. Assign the student homework of reading books that provide accurate, positive messages about homosexuality (e.g., *Is It a Choice? Answers to 300 of the Most Frequently Asked Questions about Gays and Lesbians* by Marcus; *Outing Yourself: How to Come Out as a Lesbian or Gay to Your Family, Friends, and Coworkers* by Signorile; *Coming Out: An Act of Love* by Eichberg); process reactions to the reading material in subsequent sessions.

12. Verbalize an increased understanding of the life of a homosexual or bisexual after gathering reliable information. (24, 25, 26, 27)

24. Assign the student the homework of reading books that provide accurate, positive messages about homosexuality (e.g., *Is It a Choice? Answers to 300 of the Most Frequently Asked Questions about Gays and Lesbians* by Marcus; *Outing Yourself: How to Come Out as a Lesbian or Gay to Your Family, Friends, and Coworkers* by Signorile; *Coming Out: An Act of Love* by Eichberg); process reactions to the reading material in subsequent sessions.

25. Assign the student homework of watching movies/videos that depict bisexuals or lesbian/gay men as healthy and happy (e.g., *Desert Hearts, In and Out, Jeffrey, When the Night Is Falling*); process his/her reactions in subsequent sessions.

26. Recommend homework to the student of gathering information on gay/lesbian lifestyles and/

or bisexuality by searching Internet web sites; process his/her reactions in subsequent sessions.

27. Recommend homework to the student of reviewing gay/lesbian and/or bisexual publications (e.g., *The Advocate*); process his/her reaction in subsequent sessions.

13. Attend a support group or discussion group for those wanting to disclose themselves as homosexual or bisexual. (28)

28. Suggest the student attend a coming-out support group at a local gay and lesbian community service center, AIDS Project, or other appropriate organization; process the experience after he/she has attended the group.

14. Seek out information regarding bisexual and/or gay and lesbian activities on campus. (29, 30)

29. Encourage the student to interact with bisexual, gay, or lesbian students on campus that he/she has met in classes, support groups, or other places.

30. Assist the student in identifying gay and lesbian groups and activities on campus; encourage him/her to contact these groups and process the experience.

15. Implement behavioral coping strategies for fears associated with sexual identity. (31)

31. Assist the student in developing a behavioral coping plan for his/her fear, anxiety, and distress associated with sexual identity confusion and/or coming out (e.g., learning assertiveness or social skills, initiating social contact to build a network, or making contact with a support group).

16. Identify and replace distorted self-talk that precipitates disturbing emotions concerning sexual orientation. (32, 33)

32. Assist the student in identifying his/her negative, distorted self-talk that precipitates or mediates feelings of fear, anxiety, and

distress over sexual identity confusion (e.g., "I'll never find someone who I can really fall in love with" or "My family will freak when they learn about my sexuality").

33. Teach the student realistic, positive self-talk to increase his/her sense of a more reasonable approach to dealing with fear, anxiety, and distress over sexual identity confusion (e.g., "I can find someone that I can love, and who loves me" or "My family may be shocked at first, but with time and communication, I'm sure they will be okay with this").

17. Identify and replace irrational beliefs that block effective communication with others concerning sexual orientation. (34, 35)

34. Assist the student in identifying his/her irrational beliefs that act as barriers to getting beyond the fear, anxiety, and distress over sexual identity confusion (e.g., "If this gets out, I'll be ruined"; "My friends will dump me in a flash if they ever find out"; or "I'll get kicked off the team if my coach learns about this").

35. Teach the student to rationally reframe his/her irrational beliefs to mitigate fear, anxiety, and distress over sexual identity confusion (e.g., "Today, most people really don't get too worked up over such things"; "My friends may be surprised at first, but I know my closest friend may really already know, and they have stuck with me through thick and thin"; or "My coach is tough on the field, but interpersonally, I bet she won't really care").

18. Identify one friend who is likely to have a positive reaction to disclosing homosexuality or bisexuality. (36, 37)

36. Encourage the student's identification of at least one friend who is likely to be accepting of his/her homosexuality or bisexuality.

37. Suggest that the student have casual talks about lesbian/gay rights or some similar issue to experiment with before disclosing sexual orientation to the friend.

19. Reveal sexual orientation to significant others according to written plan. (38, 39, 40)

38. Assign the student homework of writing a detailed plan on disclosing sexual orientation, including to whom it will be disclosed, where, when, and possible questions and reactions recipients might have.

39. Encourage the student's disclosure of sexual orientation to friends, roommates, and/or family according to the plan.

40. Review and process the reactions (e.g., acceptance, rejection, or shock) of significant others to the student's disclosure of homosexuality or bisexuality; provide encouragement, positive feedback, and support.

20. Identify a support system in the residence hall environment that will encourage and assist with being oneself. (41, 42)

41. Explore the peer resources (e.g., gay/lesbian discussion groups, relationship discussion groups, tolerance education meetings) available to the student in mitigating any fear, anxiety, and distress over sexual identify confusion.

42. Explore administrative staff support (e.g., resident advisor or residence director) available to provide the student suggestions in dealing with fear, anxiety, and

distress over sexual identity
confusion, especially any
potential roommate issues.

—. _____   —. _____
      _____   _____
—. _____   —. _____
      _____   _____
—. _____   —. _____
      _____   _____

DIAGNOSTIC SUGGESTIONS:

Axis I:	309.0	Adjustment Disorder with Depressed Mood
	309.28	Adjustment Disorder with Mixed Anxiety and Depressed Mood
	300.00	Anxiety Disorder NOS
	309.24	Adjustment Disorder with Anxiety
	300.4	Dysthymic Disorder
	302.85	Gender Identity Disorder
	300.02	Generalized Anxiety Disorder
	313.82	Identity Problem
	396.2x	Major Depressive Disorder, Single Episode
	296.3x	Major Depressive Disorder, Recurrent
	V62.89	Phase of Life Problem
	V61.20	Parent-Child Relational Problem
	302.9	Sexual Disorder NOS

_____   _____

_____   _____

Axis II:	301.82	Avoidant Personality Disorder
	301.83	Borderline Personality Disorder
	301.81	Narcissistic Personality Disorder
	799.9	Diagnosis Deferred
	V71.09	No Diagnosis

_____   _____

_____   _____

SUICIDAL IDEATION

BEHAVIORAL DEFINITIONS

1. Experiences unrelenting recurrent thoughts about, and preoccupation with, one's own death.
2. Experiences persistent or recurrent suicidal ideation without any plans.
3. Describes chronic suicidal ideation with a specific plan.
4. Recently attempted suicide.
5. Persistently expresses a bleak, hopeless attitude about life coupled with recent painful life events (e.g., divorce of parents; death of a close friend, loved one, or family member; severe setback in college setting, either social or academic) that support this attitude.
6. Has a positive history of suicide attempts that required professional or family/friend intervention on some level (e.g., inpatient hospitalization, outpatient care, emergency medical intervention, or close supervision by concerned others).
7. Has a positive family history of suicide.
8. Has dramatically, suddenly changed from being depressed to being upbeat and at peace without genuine resolution of conflicts.
9. Has easy access to the means of committing suicide (e.g., dangerous medications, firearms and ammunition, or illegal substances).
10. Unwilling to agree to a suicide-prevention contract or arrangement.
11. Exhibits significant social withdrawal and apathy toward classmates, friends, and/or family as well as academic and/or extracurricular activities.
12. Demonstrates marked self-destructive behavior patterns (e.g., dangerous drug or alcohol abuse, reckless driving, or assaultive) that indicate disregard for personal safety and desperate attempt to escape from emotional distress.

—. _____
_____
—. _____
_____
—. _____
_____

LONG-TERM GOALS

1. Alleviate suicidal impulses/ideation and return to the highest level of previous daily functioning.
2. Accept the appropriate level of care to address suicidal crisis.
3. Reestablish a sense of hope for self, life, academic, and social activities as well for in the future.
4. Develop adaptive methods to cope with the crisis situation that precipitated the suicidal ideation/symptoms.
5. Share emotions with family, roommates, friends, counselors, and/or other support systems during periods of distress or sadness.

—. _____
_____
—. _____
_____
—. _____
_____

SHORT-TERM OBJECTIVES

1. Discuss the relational, social, or emotional events preceding suicidal thoughts or attempts, noting the strength of the suicidal feelings, the frequency of the thoughts, and the detail of the plans. (1, 2, 3)

THERAPEUTIC INTERVENTIONS

1. Actively build a level of trust with the student using consistent eye contact, active listening, unconditional positive regard, and warm acceptance to increase his/her ability to identify and express thoughts and feelings.

2. Assist the student in identifying and clarifying the current

problems that led to feelings of self-harm in the college setting; explore the strength of suicidal urges and the details of the plan.

3. Explore the student's distress caused by living independently for the first time and how such a circumstance relates to his/her suicidal feelings.

2. Identify the personal and/or family history of mood disorder and suicidal behavior. (4, 5, 6)

4. Explore the student's history for previous episodes of suicidal ideation and attempts.

5. Explore the student's process of coping with feelings of self-harm from the past through the present.

6. Explore the student's family history for any evidence of members with affective disorders and suicidal behavior.

3. Verbalize a promise (as part of a suicide-prevention contract) to contact the counselor, the counseling center, an emergency help or crisis line, and/or appropriate family member or friend if a serious suicidal urge arises. (7, 8)

7. Obtain a promise from the student that he/she will initiate contact with the counselor, a hospital emergency room, or crisis help line if the suicidal urge becomes strong and before any self-injurious behaviors occur; provide him/her with a 24-hour emergency crisis help telephone number.

8. Share the contract of preventative action with his/her roommate, family, and/or significant others after obtaining appropriate consent from the student.

4. Cooperate with hospitalization if the suicidal urge becomes uncontrollable. (9)

9. Arrange for hospitalization if the student is judged to be at risk for uncontrollable harm to himself/herself.

5. Remove any kind of potentially lethal weapons or dangerous objects from easy access. (10)

6. Cooperate with an evaluation to determine the necessity of antidepressant medication and take medications as prescribed. (11, 12)

7. Complete a psychological evaluation to assess current emotional and cognitive functioning and aid in differential diagnosis. (13)

8. List the reasons for, reasons against, and consequences of killing self. (14, 15, 16)

10. Arrange for any potentially dangerous medications, drugs, or objects to be removed from the student's room; verify that this has been done with his/her roommate or family, if applicable.

11. Refer the student to a psychiatrist to evaluate the depth of his/her depression, level of lethality, suicide potential, and need for psychopharmacological intervention; monitor his/her follow through with completing the psychiatric evaluation.

12. Monitor the student for the therapeutic effect and/or side effects as well as compliance with the prescribed psychotropic medication; confer with the prescribing physician on a regular basis with his/her consent.

13. Conduct (or arrange for) a psychological assessment of the student's mental and emotional status; report results (after obtaining appropriate consent) to family, consulting physician, and/or the student, as appropriate.

14. Ask the student to list the reasons for, reasons against, and consequences of killing himself/herself.

15. Ask the student to write a brief autobiography that begins with early childhood and includes events that led to his/her current feelings of suicidal depression.

16. Ask the student to draw a picture of himself/herself in the

9. List and discuss positive aspects of life. (17, 18)

10. Identify and replace distorted self-talk that precipitates feelings of self-harm. (19, 20, 21)

middle of his/her current crisis situation; process the drawing.

17. Assist the student in identifying successes he/she has had while at college and sources of love and concern that exist in his/her life; ask him/her to write a list of the positive aspects of his/her life (both at and outside of the college setting).

18. Reinforce the student's ability to focus on positive attributes of himself/herself and refrain from unrealistic, negative perceptions.

19. Assist the student in identifying his/her negative, distorted self-talk that precipitates or mediates feelings of suicidal ideation and/ or feelings of self-harm (e.g., "No one really cares if I'm alive or dead"; "If I were dead, that will really show them, then they'd be sorry for the way they have treated me"; or "Things will never get better").

20. Teach the student realistic, positive self-talk to increase his/her sense of positive aspects of his/her life (e.g., "I am an intelligent person that has had some problems, but I am quite capable of learning new ways to deal with my problems more effectively" or "At times it may seem that things will never improve, but with help, support, and working at it, they will").

21. Request that the student keep a daily record of self-defeating thoughts (e.g., hopelessness, helplessness, worthlessness, catastrophizing, or negatively

predicting the future) and challenge each thought for accuracy, then replace each dysfunctional thought with one that is positive and self-enhancing.

11. Implement assertiveness and problem-solving skills to manage conflict situations. (22, 23)

22. Teach the student assertiveness skills as a means of empowerment over his/her life circumstances; encourage implementation of assertiveness, reinforcing success and redirecting failure.

23. Teach the student effective problem-solving skills: (a) problem identification or clarification in behavioral terms; (b) brainstorming of possible alternative solutions and review of the pros and cons of each; (c) selection of an alternative for implementation; (d) evaluation of the outcome in terms of satisfaction; or (e) adjustment of the solution, if necessary, to increase satisfaction.

12. Increase social interactions through implementing new social skills. (24, 25)

24. Use role-play and modeling to teach the student social skills that can be used to initiate and maintain social relationships; assign initiation of one contact per day, reinforcing success, and redirecting failure.

25. Assist the student in identifying opportunities for building his/her social network (e.g., campus activities, clubs or organizations, intramurals, entertainment, church or synagogue activities, or dorm gatherings); assign him/her to attend two per week.

13. Implement behavioral and preventative coping strategies to overcome feelings of self-harm. (26, 27)

14. Identify and replace irrational beliefs that block effective problem-solving and/or emotional expression that may lead to feelings of self-harm. (28, 29, 30)

26. Teach the student adaptive reactions to his/her suicidal triggers (e.g., discuss with roommate or counselor or go for a run or some other safe, physically exerting activity).

27. Assist the student in developing preventative strategies for avoiding suicidal ideation (e.g., more physical exercise, greater engagement in academic work/classes, less internal focus, increased social involvement, engagement in extracurricular activity, or more frequent expression of feelings in an appropriate manner); encourage implementation of these strategies and monitor for follow through.

28. Assist the student in identifying his/her irrational beliefs that act as barriers to effectively coping with feelings of suicidal ideation and/or feelings of self-harm (e.g., "I'd be better off dead" or "There is no other way to get out of this pain than to die").

29. Teach the student to rationally reframe his/her irrational beliefs to remove barriers to feelings of suicidal ideation and/or feelings of self-harm (e.g., "I do get depressed, but there are also times following such moods where I seem to have more hope" or "There are some people here at college who do really seem to care about me").

30. Identify and confront catastrophizing tendencies in the student's cognitive processing, allowing for a more realistic

perspective of hope in the face of painful circumstances.

15. Identify a support system in the residence-hall environment that will encourage and assist during times of experiencing feelings of self-harm. (31)

31. Assist the student in identifying administrative staff support (e.g., resident advisor, residence director) available to provide him/her with help if feelings of suicidal ideation and/or self-harm become difficult to manage.

16. Participate in family therapy sessions to identify feelings and resolve conflicts related to family members. (32, 33, 34)

32. Conduct family therapy sessions to identify familial factors contributing to the student's suicidal ideation.

33. Probe the student's feelings of despair related to his/her family relationships.

34. Meet with the student's significant others, roommates, family, and/or friends, to assess their understanding of the causes for the student's distress.

17. Family members verbalize an understanding of the student's suicidal crisis. (35, 36, 37, 38)

35. Educate the student's family about the signs of depression and methods of offering emotional support to the student.

36. Conduct family therapy sessions to promote communication of the student's feelings of sadness, hurt, and/or anger.

37. Instruct family members, with appropriate consents, to be sensitive to the reoccurrence of suicidal ideation in the student (e.g., suicidal threat, preoccupation with death, or significant social withdrawal) and provide methods of therapeutic response (e.g., contacting the counselor and/or emergency services).

38. Notify the student's family, roommates, and/or appropriate

significant others of the student's suicidal ideation; request a 24-hour suicide watch until the crisis subsides, if appropriate.

18. Demonstrate improved social functioning and self-care by regularly eating nutritious meals, attending classes, sleeping six to eight hours per night, and socializing. (39, 40, 41, 42)

39. Emphasize the importance to the student of following through with daily living activities, exercising, maintaining social contacts, and reinforcing good nutritional intake.

40. Positively reinforce the student for arising in a timely manner and engaging in the routine activities of the day on campus and in classes.

41. Teach the student relaxation methods (e.g., progressive muscle relaxation, guided, or visual imagery) to aide in reducing stress during the day and inducing sleep at night.

42. Monitor the student's sleep patterns and educate him/her on biofeedback, self-hypnosis, and other methods of body control to facilitate restorative, restful sleep.

19. Verbalize an absence of suicidal ideation incidents and of having hope in self and for the future. (20, 27, 29, 43)

20. Teach the student realistic, positive self-talk to increase his/her sense of positive aspects of his/her life (e.g., "I am an intelligent person that has had some problems, but I am quite capable of learning new ways to deal with my problems more effectively" or "At times it may seem that things will never improve, but with help, support, and working at it, they will").

27. Assist the student in developing preventative strategies for avoiding suicidal ideation (e.g.,

more physical exercise, greater engagement in academic work/ classes, less internal focus, increased social involvement, engagement in extracurricular activity, or more frequent expression of feelings in an appropriate manner); encourage implementation of these strategies and monitor for follow through.

29. Teach the student to rationally reframe his/her irrational beliefs to remove barriers to feelings of suicidal ideation and/or feelings of self-harm (e.g., "I do get depressed, but there are also times following such moods where I seem to have more hope" or "There are some people here at college who do really seem to care about me").

43. Monitor and reinforce the student's statements of hope for the future.

—. _____
_____

—. _____
_____

—. _____
_____

—. _____
_____

—. _____
_____

—. _____
_____

DIAGNOSTIC SUGGESTIONS:

Axis I: 296.2x   Major Depressive Disorder, Single Episode
296.3x   Major Depressive Disorder, Recurrent
296.xx   Bipolar I Disorder
300.4   Dysthymic Disorder
296.89   Bipolar II Disorder

_____   _____

_____   _____

Axis II: 301.83   Borderline Personality Disorder
799.9   Diagnosis Deferred
V71.09   No Diagnosis

_____   _____

_____   _____

TIME MANAGEMENT

BEHAVIORAL DEFINITIONS

1. Consistently arrives late for class, employment, meetings, and social engagements.
2. Unrealistically short assessment of the time required to complete tasks.
3. Fails to create advance plans to accomplish tasks in a timely manner to meet deadlines.
4. Does not commit to plans for completion of projects, papers, readings, or other tasks.
5. Does not complete work by the deadline or due date.
6. Completes assignments well past the deadline or never completes them.
7. Inaccurately perceives how time is spent.
8. Procrastinates in the face of negative effects on academic achievement.
9. Lacks timeliness, creating a strain on interpersonal relationships.
10. Does not respect others' time as evidenced by consistently being late after committing to a meeting time.

___. _____

_____

___. _____

_____

___. _____

_____

LONG-TERM GOALS

1. Develop a realistic assessment of how time is typically spent.
2. View successful time management as a commitment to self.

3. Identify particular roadblocks to successful time management.
4. Employ specific strategies to overcome time-management problems.
5. Increase timeliness as a contributor to improved academic performance.
6. Demonstrate respect for others' time and reduce strain on interpersonal relationships.

—. _____
   _____
   _____

—. _____
   _____
   _____

—. _____
   _____

SHORT-TERM OBJECTIVES

THERAPEUTIC INTERVENTIONS

1. Describe the nature and consequences of own time-management deficits. (1, 2, 3)

1. Ask the student to recount specific incidents that exemplify his/her difficulties in effectively managing time.

2. Assist the student in identifying the negative consequences for himself/herself and others of poor time management; ask him/her to list those that he/she has experienced.

3. Explore the student's emotional and behavioral responses to the negative consequences of his/her poor time management.

2. Keep a record to assess time-management patterns. (4, 5, 6)

4. Assign a time journal for the student to log all activity in 30-minute segments for at least two full weeks.

5. Review each day of the student's time journal, asking him/her to identify the problem areas of any given day.

6. Assist the student in recognizing the time-management

patterns (e.g., procrastination, inefficiency, slow pace, distractibility, or lack of planning) that are causing him/her the greatest difficulty and/or losses.

3. Develop a plan to address time-management issues. (7, 8, 9, 10)

7. Ask the student to compile a list of commitments and responsibilities over the next two weeks, identifying the places where current time-management patterns are likely to cause problems.

8. Ask the student to rank and order time-management problems to be addressed, placing the patterns that most interfere with effective functioning at the top.

9. Assist the student in identifying and recording a remedy for each of his/her listed time-management problems; solicit a commitment that the remedies will be implemented in the next two weeks.

10. Provide the student with readings on time management techniques (e.g., *Procrastination* by Burka and Yuen, "Take Charge of Your Time" in *Learning Skills for College and Career* by Hettich) and ask him/her to select the techniques that will address his/her key concerns; process ideas garnered from the reading and obtain a commitment for implementation.

4. Identify patterns of time-wasting behavior. (4, 11)

4. Assign a time journal for the student to log all activity in 30-minute segments for at least two full weeks.

11. Analyze the student's completed time journal with him/her, paying particular attention to his/her personal set of time enhancers and time wasters, and brainstorm ways to increase the use of the enhancers and eliminate the wasters.

5. List task and assignment commitments that are required to be completed in the near future. (12, 13)

12. Ask the student to create a list of all school, work, organizational, and personal commitments for the semester and post them on a large calendar that he/she will bring to each session.

13. Review the student's syllabi, noting all exams, papers, presentations, and other major assignments due for all courses.

6. Employ tools necessary for the timely accomplishment of large tasks or projects. (14, 15, 16)

14. Encourage the student to write down his/her goal for the outcome of each exam and assignment during the time period as well as a written list of planned activities necessary to achieve these academic goals.

15. Ask the student to put the planned time management activities into a time line and transcribe them on his/her calendar.

16. Assist the student in determining ways in which weekly time journals can accurately reflect calendar goals and activities (i.e., what were the situations or issues that resulted in discrepancies between the number of study, research, or writing hours planned [calendar/time line] and the number that actually occurred [weekly time journal]).

7. Identify and replace the thoughts and emotions that

17. Encourage the student to discuss personal successes, failures, and

trigger procrastination. (17, 18, 19)

the role procrastination has played in forming his/her self concept.

18. Using positive self-talk and affirmation, help the student reframe the difficult feelings prompted by failure.

19. Encourage the student to identify the emotions that trigger procrastination (e.g., need for perfection, or fear of failure, critical review by others, or success) and write a script of proactive responses to limit the amount of time lost to this behavior.

8. Implement organizational skills necessary for task/goal accomplishment. (20, 21, 22)

20. Ask the student to describe a workspace that is conducive to his/her academic studying and achievement; assist him/her in deciding to establish and maintain this space.

21. Help the student identify and acquire the tools (e.g., folders, files, computer disks, notebooks, or reading and writing materials) necessary to maintain a sense of organization when approaching a task.

22. Refer the student to his/her calendar to prioritize work.

9. Verbalize an acceptance of accountability for task completion and goal attainment. (23, 24, 25)

23. Provide the student with information on decision-making styles, asking him/her to identify the pros and cons of his/her particular style (e.g., Impulsive Decider: "Decide now, think later"; Fatalistic Decider: "Whatever will be will be"; Compliant Decider: "Anything you say, whatever you want"; Delaying Decider: "I'll think about it later"; Agonizing

Decider: "There's too much information to consider, I just can't make up my mind"; Intuitive Decider: "It just feels like the right decision"; Play-It-Safe Decider: "I'll take the choice that requires little to no risk"; Planning Decider: "I am responsible for my own life, I am in charge of me" from Dinklage, as referenced at www.byu.edu/ccc/career/decision.sthml).

24. Explore the student's recent task/goal accomplishment decisions, highlighting situations in which he/she identifies with the victim-of-circumstance role.

25. Guide the student in refusing the role of victim and embracing ownership of his/her choices and the corresponding consequences.

10. Contact those people damaged by poor time management to make amends. (26, 27, 28)

26. Encourage the student to identify the people who have been negatively affected by his/her poor time-management decisions.

27. Suggest that the student contact these people with the goal of making amends and putting these relationships on a healthier and more equitable track.

28. Assign the creation of a template for the conversations to make amends and participate in role-plays with the student of these conversations; urge him/her to implement these contacts and then process the outcome.

11. Keep a journal of positive time-management activities and the consequences. (29, 30)

29. Ask the student to journal about the positive changes that have occurred in his/her life in

response to improved time-management skills.

30. Suggest that the student maintain a time journal and calendar for a minimum of six months to foster and solidify newly developed time management skills.

—. _____   —. _____
_____   _____
—. _____   —. _____
_____   _____
—. _____   —. _____
_____   _____

DIAGNOSTIC SUGGESTIONS:

Axis I: 799.9   Diagnosis Deferred
              V71.09 No Diagnosis

          _____ _____
          _____ _____

Axis II: 799.9   Diagnosis Deferred
              V71.09 No Diagnosis

          _____ _____
          _____ _____

Appendix A

SAMPLE CHAPTER WITH QUANTIFIED LANGUAGE

ACADEMIC UNDERACHIEVEMENT

BEHAVIORAL DEFINITIONS[*]

1. Thoughts about assignments and/or tests provoke feelings of anxiety and prevent optimum academic performance that occur _____ times per day.
2. Fear of failure leads to avoidance of allocating the necessary time and effort to studying that occurs _____ times per day (or that occurs _____ times per course).
3. Unable or unwilling to employ study skills necessary for academic achievement at the college level (e.g., note-taking in class, underlining and summarizing reading, or test-taking strategies) that occurs _____ times per day.
4. Decline in academic performance evidenced by _____ that occurs in response to environmental stress (e.g., parents' divorce, death of a loved one, loss of a relationship, or roommate conflict).
5. Maintains unrealistically high expectations for academic achievement as evidenced by _____.

---

[*]*Note:* For each behavioral definition look for or include valid reports of differential levels of occurrence (both higher and lower) between certain times of the day; with certain days of the week; with certain friends, courses, and faculty; and under certain circumstances.

6. Unable to meet family demands for academic performance as evidenced by _____ .
7. Lacks time-management and/or goal-setting skills as evidenced by _____ .
8. Learning style conflicts with the typical instructional methods used by college professors as evidenced by _____ and occurs _____ times per day (or occurs _____ times per course).
9. Learning disability impedes/prevents academic success as evidenced by _____ .
10. Experiences difficulty remaining attentive in lectures and classroom discussions and occurs _____ times per day (or occurs _____ times per course).
11. Class attendance and/or participation are below the level necessary for academic success as evidenced by _____ and occurs _____ times per day (or occurs _____ times per course).
12. Family, work, and social commitments reduce the amount of time available for academic work to an unacceptable level, as evidenced by _____ and occurs _____ times per day.

__. _____
   _____
__. _____
   _____
__. _____
   _____

LONG-TERM GOALS

1. Learn and implement stress-management skills to reduce academic performance anxiety.
2. Hone study skills that are necessary for academic achievement in college.
3. Employ time-management and goal-setting skills necessary for academic success.
4. Develop realistic expectations about academic ability to benchmark academic achievement.
5. Significantly improve class attendance and in-class participation.
6. Identify learning disabilities (if any) and create and implement an educational plan for academic success.
7. Create strategies to effectively manage the expectations of significant others for academic achievement.

—. _____
_____
—. _____
_____
—. _____
_____

SHORT-TERM OBJECTIVES	THERAPEUTIC INTERVENTIONS
1. By _____ (enter date), the student will begin to clarify the facts, beliefs, and feelings about academic ability and performance and discuss in session. (1, 2, 3)	1. Explore the student's beliefs about his/her academic ability and performance; review his/her history of academic performance (e.g., GPA, grade transcript, or number of classes enrolled in per term).
	2. Identify the key factors that have combined to create the student's beliefs about his/her academic ability and performance (e.g., parental pressure, teachers' feedback, academic history, or personal/career ambitions).
	3. Help the student identify and clarify the feelings (e.g., anxiety, doubt, frustration, guilt, joy, pride, or shame) generated by his/her beliefs about academic ability and performance.
2. By _____ (enter date), the student will explore the impact of his/her personal belief system on academic behaviors. (4, 5, 6)	4. Ask the student to list, as specifically as possible, his/her belief statements (or expectations) about his/her academic ability and performance (e.g., "I must get all As," or "I am not going to do well in math anyway, so there is no point to studying").

5. Help the student evaluate each of his/her beliefs about his/her academic performance using the questions, "Is this a reasonable (rational) expectation?" and "Is this an achievable expectation?" as criteria.

6. Assist the student in recognizing the connection between irrational and/or unachievable academic beliefs or expectations and the emotional struggles and academic problems he/she is currently experiencing.

3. By _____ (enter date), the student will start to restructure academic expectations, making them rational and conducive to constructive academic behaviors. (7, 8, 9, 10)

7. Assign the student homework of revising his/her belief statements, making each statement more reasonable and achievable (e.g., "I am committed to maintaining a 2.8 to 3.5 GPA each semester" or "I can improve my math performance and will do so by utilizing the learning assistance resources provided on campus").

8. Review the student's belief statements and discuss similarities to and differences from the original unreasonable statements.

9. Ask the student to identify and record positive emotional reactions and academic behaviors that each revised belief statement would generate.

10. Assign the student homework of creating a plan of action to incorporate and prioritize positive academic behaviors (e.g., "I will use Sunday evenings to review the academic demands of the week ahead and make necessary adjustments to my schedule"; "I will immediately

discuss problem grades on homework, tests, and/or papers with my professors"; "I will seek the assistance of the tutoring center if I am having ongoing difficulty with a particular class") according to his/her current academic needs.

4. By _____ (enter date), the student will utilize learning assistance resources offered by the campus to improve study skills and habits. (11, 12)

11. Encourage the student to register for courses that teach study skills or to attend workshops or programs that focus on developing reading, listening, note-taking, test-taking, or other effective academic learning strategies.

12. Refer the student to campus-based peer or professional tutors for assistance in understanding specific course content essential to the successful completion of his/her current classes.

5. By _____ (enter date), the student will analyze time commitments through journaling. (13, 14, 15)

13. Ask the student to list weekly academic, job, social, and personal commitments and the corresponding amounts of time required to accomplish each one, paying particular attention to class attendance and completion of academic work.

14. Assign a time journal to log all student activities in 30-minute segments for one full week (see Time Management chapter in this *Planner*).

15. Compare the student's original list of time commitments to his/her time journal, asking him/her to identify activities where there are discrepancies between the projected time required by each activity and the actual time spent.

6. By _____ (enter date), the student will maintain a schedule that encourages academic achievement by successfully balancing academic, work, social, and personal commitments of time and energy. (16, 17)

16. Assist the student in creating a schedule for the next week that reallocates time spent in areas where discrepancies existed and produce a more balanced and productive week (see Time Management chapter in this *Planner*).

17. Encourage the student to use a structured schedule each week to guide his/her time usage and assist in the achievement of academic behaviors outlined in his/her plan of action.

7. By _____ (enter date), the student will cooperate with an evaluation for the presence of a learning disability. (18)

18. If appropriate, suggest that the student explore the possibility of learning disabilities causing his/her performance deficits and refer him/her for the testing necessary for an accurate diagnosis.

8. By _____ (enter date), the student will implement a learning plan that incorporates the strengths of his/her personal learning style. (19, 20, 21)

19. Suggest that the student investigate various learning styles (e.g., Kolb's Learning Style Inventory, Myers-Briggs Type Indicator, or similar inventories can be used) to determine his/her learning style.

20. Ask the student to work with a learning-assistance counselor to develop an individualized learning plan to identify specific classroom and study behaviors that are most effective with his/her learning style and/or learning disabilities.

21. Incorporate the suggestions from the individualized learning plan into the student's plan of action and review his/her progress at each session to ensure that learning skills are being

9. By _____ (enter date), the student shall demonstrate skills necessary to communicate effectively in writing. (22, 23)

10. By _____ (enter date), the student will increase the frequency of verbal participation in the classroom learning process. (24, 25, 26)

11. By _____ (enter date), the student will gather the support of significant others by sharing academic expectations, learning plans, and activities. (27, 28)

12. By _____ (enter date), the student will report a sense of

developed and learning objectives are being met.

22. Refer the student to the campus's writing clinic and/or peer tutoring center for ongoing assistance with writing assignments.

23. Encourage the student to identify a friend who will act as his/her editor for any assignments that are not reviewed by a tutor.

24. Contract with the student to speak at least once per class in each course that allows or encourages classroom participation.

25. Suggest that the student become involved in at least one study group where active participation is the norm.

26. Ask the student to register for a speech or group communications course to demystify the process of and reduce his/her anxiety about speaking in front of others.

27. Assist the student in developing talking points about the changes in his/her academic expectations and behaviors that he/she can use in discussions with significant others, and explore the corresponding impact on the expectations of significant others.

28. Encourage the student to provide significant others with progress updates that will keep them aware of his/her academic struggles and successes.

10. Assign the student homework of creating a plan of action to

self-efficacy regarding academic performance. (10, 17, 29)

incorporate and prioritize positive academic behaviors (e.g., "I will use Sunday evenings to review the academic demands of the week ahead and make necessary adjustments to my schedule"; "I will immediately discuss problem grades on home-work, tests, and/or papers with my professors"; and "I will seek the assistance of the tutoring center if I am having ongoing difficulty with a particular class") according to his/her current academic needs.

17. Encourage the student to use a structured schedule each week to guide his/her time usage and assist in the achievement of academic behaviors outlined in his/her plan of action.

29. Review the student's progress on his/her plan of action weekly for the remainder of the semester and biweekly to monthly during the next semester to ensure that new behaviors and skills are operationalized.

13. By _____ (enter date), the student will identify the debilitating effects of high anxiety levels on academic performance with specific examples of courses and/or professors. (30, 31)

30. Teach the student about the debilitating effects of anxiety on academic performance (e.g., increased distractibility, reduced ability to recall material, increased strength of negative outcome expectations, preoccu-pation with physiological aspects of anxiety [increased heart rate, perspiration, shallow breathing, or dizziness], or fatigue from muscle tension and sleep disturbance).

31. Ask the student to list how he/she perceives anxiety is making a

14. By _____ (enter date), the student will identify and address the suspected causes of performance anxiety. (32, 33)

negative impact of his/her academic performance.

32. Assist the student in identifying the causes of his/her debilitating performance anxiety (e.g., unreasonable personal beliefs or expectations about academic performance, unreasonable expectations from parents, past failure experiences, recent adjustment problems to life on campus, lack of tutorial assistance for new and difficult material, or poor study skills or time management).

33. Develop a plan to address the identified causes of the student's performance anxiety (e.g., replace irrational beliefs about academic performance, confront parental expectations directly, apply problem solving to campus life issues of conflict, access campus-based tutoring services, implement effective study skills or time-management procedures).

15. By _____ (enter date), the student will implement relaxation techniques to reduce test-taking stress, demonstrating a ___ % reduction in _____ weeks. (34, 35, 36)

34. Teach the student relaxation skills (e.g., deep muscle release, deep breathing, or progressive relaxation) to implement at times of high test anxiety or general performance stress.

35. Teach the student about positive imagery (e.g., imagining a relaxing scene of laying on a beach under the warm sun, full and clear recall of facts during a test situation, successful enactment of skills in front of a group) to induce calm, relaxation, and a sense of peace during times of high test or performance anxiety.

36. Use role-playing to help the student apply relaxation and positive imagery skills to specific debilitating performance anxiety situations.

16. By _____ (enter date), the student will report an increased (by a ___ % difference in _____ weeks) confidence in his/her ability following implementation of effective study skills as preparation for tests. (11, 37, 38)

11. Encourage the student to register for courses that teach study skills or attend workshops or programs that focus on developing reading, listening, note-taking, test-taking, or other effective academic learning strategies.

37. Review the student's implementation of effective study skills; reinforce success and redirect failure.

38. Reassure the student that adequate preparation using effective study methods and prudent time management (see Time Management chapter in this *Planner*) will result in good academic performance as anxiety is reduced.

__. _____   __. _____
  _____   _____
__. _____   __. _____
  _____   _____
__. _____   __. _____
  _____   _____

DIAGNOSTIC SUGGESTIONS:

Axis I:

300.02	Generalized Anxiety Disorder	
300.00	Anxiety Disorder NOS	
309.24	Adjustment Disorder with Anxiety	
314.01	Attention-Deficit/Hyperactivity Disorder, Combined Type	
V62.3	Academic Problem	
799.9	Diagnosis Deferred	
V71.09	No Diagnosis	

_____   _____

_____   _____

Axis II:

799.9	Diagnosis Deferred
V71.09	No Diagnosis

_____   _____

_____   _____

Appendix B

BIBLIOTHERAPY SUGGESTIONS

Introduction

Chickering, A. W. (1969). *Education and Identity.* San Francisco, CA: Jossey-Bass.

Chickering, A. W. and Reisser, L. (1993). *Education and Identity.* San Francisco, CA: Jossey-Bass

Erickson, E. H. (1963). *Childhood and Society* (2nd ed.). New York: W.W. Norton & Company.

Erickson, E. H. (1968). *Identity: Youth and Crisis.* New York: W.W. Norton & Company.

Erickson, E. H. (1980). *Identity and Life Cycle.* New York: W.W. Norton & Company.

Marcia, J. E. (1966). "Development and Validation of Ego-Identity Status." *Journal of Personality and Social Psychology, 3,* 551–558.

Marcia, J. E. (1980). "Identity in Adolescent." In J. Adelson (Ed.), *Handbook of Adolescent Psychology* (pp. 159–187). New York: John Wiley & Sons, Inc.

Parks, S. D. (2000). *Big Questions, Worthy Dreams.* San Francisco, CA: Jossey-Bass.

Abusive Relationships

Gray, J. (2002). *Men, Women and Relationships: Making Peace with the Opposite Sex.* New York: Quill.

Lerner, H. G. (1990). *The Dance of Intimacy.* New York: HarperPerennial.

Middelton-Moz, J. (1990). *Shame and Guilt: Masters of Disguise.* Deerfield Beach, FL: Health Communications.

Munsch, R., and Martchenko, M. (2003). *The Paper Bag Princess.* Buffalo, NY: Annick Press.

Norwood, R. (1997). *Women Who Love Too Much.* New York: Pocket Books.

Academic Major Selection

Malnig, L., Case, E., and Malnig, A. (1984). *What Can I Do with a Major in . . . ? How to Choose and Use Your College Major.* Ridgefield, NJ: Abbot Press.

Phifer, P. (1993). *College Majors and Careers.* Garrett Park, MD: Garrett Park Press.

Academic Underachievement

Hettich, P. (1998). *Learning Skills for College and Career*. Pacific Grove, CA: Brooks/Cole Publishing Company.

Juster, N. (1996). *The Phantom Tollbooth*. New York: Random House.

McCall, R. B., Evahn, C., and Kratzer, L. (1992). *High School Underachievers: What Do They Achieve as Adults?* London, UK: Sage Publications.

Antisocial Behavior

Bradshaw, J. (1988). *Healing the Shame*. Deerfield Beach, FL: Health Communications.

Pittman, F. (1998). *Grow Up!* New York: Golden Books.

Smedes, L. (1991). *Forgive and Forget*. San Francisco: HarperSanFrancisco.

Williams, R., and Williams, V. (1993). *Anger Kills*. New York: Time Books.

Career Choice Confusion

Carter, C. (1999). *Majoring in the Rest of Your Life*. New York: Farrar, Straus, and Giroux.

Eikleberry, C. (1999). *The Career Guide for Creative and Unconventional People*. Berkeley, CA: Ten Speed Press.

Gabler, L. R. (2000). *Career Exploration on the Internet*. Chicago, IL: Ferguson Publishing Company.

Mitchell, J. S. (1994). *The College Board Guide to Jobs and Career Planning*. New York: College Board Publications.

Montross, D. H., Liebowitz, Z. B., and Shinkman, C. J. (1995). *Real Jobs, Real People: Reflecting Your Interests in the World of Work*. Palo Alto, CA: Davies-Black Publishing.

Chemical Dependence/Abuse

Fanning, P., and O'Neil, J. (1996). *The Addiction Workbook*. Oakland, CA: New Harbinger Publications.

Johnson, V. (1980). *I'll Quit Tomorrow*. New York: Harper & Row.

Childhood Abuse

Bass, E., and Davis, L. (1988). *The Courage to Heal*. New York: Harper & Row.

Bradshaw, J. (1988). *Healing the Shame That Binds You*. Deerfield Beach, FL: Health Communications.

Brady, M. (1992). *Beyond Survival: A Writing Journal for Healing Childhood Sexual Abuse*. New York: HarperCollins.

Clarke, J. I., and Dawson, C. (1998). *Growing Up Again.* Center City, MN: Hazelden.

Gil, E. (1988). *Outgrowing the Pain.* Rockville, MD: Launch Press.

Hunter, M. (1990). *Abused Boys: The Neglected Victims of Sexual Abuse.* New York: Fawcett Columbine.

Katherine, A. (1993). *Boundaries: When You End and I Begin.* New York: Simon & Schuster.

Simon, S. B., and Simon, S. (1990). *Forgiveness: How to Make Peace with Your Past and Get on with Your Life.* New York: Warner Books.

Witfield, C. L. (1994). *Boundaries and Relationships.* Deerfield Beach, FL: Health Communications.

Depression

Alberti, R., and Emmons, M. (2001). *Your Perfect Right: Assertiveness and Equality in Your Life and Relationships.* San Luis Obispo, CA: Impact Publishers.

Burns, D. (1989). *The Feeling Good Handbook.* New York: Blume.

Helmstetter, S. (1986). *What to Say When You Talk to Yourself.* New York: Fine Communications.

Leith, L. (1998). *Exercising Your Way to Better Mental Health.* Morgantown, WV: Fitness Information Technology.

Smith, M. (1975). *When I Say No, I Feel Guilty.* New York: Bantam.

Diversity Acceptance

Briggs Myers, I. (1997). *Gifts Differing.* Palo Alto, CA: Consulting Psychologists Press.

Light, R. J. (2001). *Making the Most of College.* Cambridge, MA: Harvard University Press.

Eating Disorders

Fairburn, C. (1995). *Overcoming Binge Eating.* New York: Guilford Publications.

Siegel, M., Brisman, J., and Weinshel, M. (1997). *Surviving an Eating Disorder.* San Francisco: HarperCollins.

Family Relationship Conflicts

Bower, S. A., and Bower, G. H. (1991). *Asserting Yourself.* Cambridge, MA: Perseus Books.

Clarke, J. I., and Dawson, C. (1998). *Growing Up Again.* Center City, MN: Hazelden.

Forward, S., and Buck, C. (2002). *Toxic Parents.* New York: Bantam Books.

Friel, J., and Friel, L. (1990). *An Adult Child's Guide to What's "Normal."* Deerfield Beach, FL: Health Communications.

Kerr, M. E. (1988). *Family Evaluation: An Approach Based on Bowen Theory.* New York: W.W. Norton & Company.

Lerner, H. G. (1990). *The Dance of Intimacy.* New York: HarperPerennial.

Lerner, H. G. (2001). *The Dance of Anger.* New York: Quill Publications.

Pipher, M. (1997). *The Shelter of Each Other: Rebuilding Our Families.* New York: Ballantine Books.

Tannen, D. (2001). *I Only Say This Because I Love You.* New York: Ballantine Books.

Financial Stress

Arndt, T., and Ricchini, J. (2003). *Life After Graduation: Financial Advice and Money Saving Tips.* Alexandria, VA: Life After Graduation.

Baker, M. (2000). *The Debt-Free Graduate: How to Survive College Without Going Broke.* Franklin Lakes, NJ: Career Press.

Braitman, E. (1998). *Dollars and Sense for College Students.* New York: Princeton Review Publishing.

Peterson's. (2004). *Peterson's Scholarships, Grants, and Prizes 2004.* Princeton, NJ: Peterson's.

Schlatchter, G. (2003). *How to Find Out about Financial Aid and Funding, 2003–2005.* El Dorado Hills, CA: Reference Service Press.

Graduation Anxiety

Beck, M. (2001). *Finding Your Own North Star.* New York: Three Rivers Press.

Burka, J. B., and Yuen, L. M. (1983). *Procrastination.* Cambridge, MA: Perseus Books.

Burns, D. D. (1993). *Ten Days to Self-Esteem.* New York: Quill.

Davis, M., Eshelman, E., and McKay, M. (2000). *The Relaxation and Stress Reduction Workbook.* Oakland, CA: New Harbinger Publications, Inc.

Helmstetter, S. (1990). *What to Say When You Talk to Yourself.* New York: Pocket Books.

Hettich, P., and Helkowski, C. (2005). *Connect College to Career: A Student's Guide to Work and Life Transitions.* Belmont, CA: Wadsworth.

Luppert, E. (1998). *Rules of the Road: Surviving Your First Job Out of School.* New York: Berkley Publishing Group.

Margolis, G. (1980). Learning to Leave: Problems of Graduating. *Journal of American College Health Association, 28.*

Robbins, A., and Wilner, A. (2001). *Quarterlife Crisis: The Unique Challenge of Life in Your Twenties.* New York: Tarcher/Putnam.

Sullivan, R. (2002). *Getting Your Foot in the Door When You Don't Have a Leg to Stand On.* New York: Contemporary Books.

Grief/Loss

Kushner, H. (1981). *When Bad Things Happen to Good People.* New York: Schocken Books.

Schiff, N. (1977). *The Bereaved Parent*. New York: Crown Publication.

Smedes, L. (1982). *How Can It Be All Right When Everything Is All Wrong*. San Francisco: HarperSanFrancisco.

Smedes, L. (1991). *Forgive and Forget: Healing the Hurts We Don't Deserve*. San Francisco: HarperSanFrancisco.

Smedes, L. (1993). *The Art of Forging*. New York: Ballantine Books.

Westberg, G. (1962). *Good Grief*. Philadelphia: Augsburg Fortress Press.

Homesickness/Emancipation Issues

Anderson, H., and Mitchell, K. R. (1993). *Leaving Home*. Louisville, KY: Westminster/John Knox Press.

Coelho, P. (1998). *The Alchemist*. New York: HarperPerennial.

Johnson, S. (1998). *Who Moved My Cheese?* New York: Putnam.

March. J. (1994). *A Primer on Decision Making: How Decisions Happen*. New York: The Free Press.

Levoy, G. (1998). *Callings: Finding and Following an Authentic Life*. New York: Three Rivers Press.

Ricchini, J., and Arndt, T. (2002). *Life During College: Valuable Advice & Tips for Success*. Alexandria, VA: Life After Graduation.

Intimacy/Commitment Issues

Covey, S. (1990). *The Seven Habits of Highly Effective People*. New York: Simon & Schuster.

Gray, J. (2002). *Men, Women and Relationships*. New York: Quill.

Kasl, C. (1999). *If the Buddha Dated*. New York: Penguin Putnam.

Kerr, M. E. (1988). *Family Evaluation: An Approach Based on Bowen Theory*. New York: W.W. Norton & Company.

Lerner, H. G. (1990). *The Dance of Intimacy*. New York: HarperPerennial.

Louden, J. (1994). *The Couple's Comfort Book*. San Francisco, CA: HarperSanFrancisco.

McCann, E., and Shannon, D. (1985). *The Two Step: The Dance Toward Intimacy*. New York: Grove Press.

McFarland, E., and Saywell, J. (2001). *If . . .* New York: Villard Books.

Mountain Dreamer, O. (1999). *The Invitation*. San Francisco, CA: HarperSanFrancisco.

Piver, S. (2000). *The Hard Questions*. New York: Penguin Putnam.

Sternberg, R. (1988). *The Triangle of Love*. New York: Basic Books.

Tannen, D. (1990). *You Just Don't Understand: Men and Women in Conversation*. New York: Ballantine Books.

Learning/Physical Disabilities

Clayton, L., and Morrison, J. (1999). *Coping with a Learning Disability*. New York: Rosen Publishing Group.

Disability Resource Directory: http://www.kansas.net/~cbaslock/olc_dl.html.

Ryan, D. J. (2000). *Job Search Book for People with Disabilities.* Indianapolis, IN: JIST Works.

Weiss, L. (1997). *Attention Deficit Disorder in Adults.* Dallas, TX: Taylor Publishing Company.

Yahoo! Disabilities Directory: http://d2.dir.dcn/yahoo.com/society_and_culture/disabilities.

Loneliness

Antony, M., and Swinson, R. (2000). *The Shyness & Social Anxiety Workbook: Proven Techniques for Overcoming Your Fears.* New York: New Harbinger Publications.

Butler, G. (2001). *Overcoming Social Anxiety and Shyness: A Self-Help Guide Using Cognitive Behavior Techniques.* New York: New York University Press.

Lerner, H. G. (1990). *The Dance of Intimacy.* New York: HarperPerennial.

Pregnancy

Planned Parenthood: www.plannedparenthood.org.

Smith, S., and Smith, C. (1992). *College Student's Health Guide.* Los Altos, CA: Westchester Publishing Company.

Psychotic Break

Carter, R., and Golant, S. (1998). *Helping Someone with Mental Illness: A Compassionate Guide for Family, Friends, and Caregivers.* New York: Time Books.

Torrey, M. D., and Fuller, E. (1988). *Surviving Schizophrenia: A Family Manual.* New York: Harper & Row.

Rape/Sexual Assault Victim

Baty, K. (2003). *A Girl's Gotta Do What A Girl's Gotta Do.* New York: Rodale.

Brownmiller, S. (1993). *Against Our Will: Women, Men and Rape.* New York: Fawcett Columbine.

Hasselbrack, A. (1999). *Extra-Curricular: A Novel of Rape on Campus.* College Park, MD: Anne M. Hasselbrack.

Scott, K. (1993). *Sexual Assault: Will I Ever Feel OK Again?* Minneapolis, MN: Bethany House Publishers.

Warshaw, R. (1994). *I Never Called It Rape.* New York: HarperPerennial.

Roommate Conflicts

Bower, S. A., and Bower, G. H. (1991). *Asserting Yourself.* Cambridge, MA: Perseus Books.

Katherine, A. (1993). *Boundaries: Where You End and I Begin.* New York: Simon & Schuster.

Lieberman, D. J. (2002). *Make Peace With Anyone.* New York: St. Martin's Griffin.

Pachter, B. (2000). *The Power of Positive Confrontation.* New York: Marlowe & Company.

Whitfield, C. (1990). *A Gift to Myself.* Deerfield Beach, FL: Health Communications.

Self-Esteem Deficit

Burns, D. (1993). *Ten Days to Self-Esteem!* New York: William Morrow.

Helmstetter, S. (1986). *What to Say When You Talk to Yourself.* New York: Fine Communications.

Shapiro, L. (1993). *Building Blocks to Self Esteem.* King of Prussia, PA: Center for Applied Psychology.

Self-Mutiliation/Borderline Personality

Cudney, M., and Handy, R. (1993). *Self-Defeating Behaviors.* San Francisco: HarperSanFrancisco.

Linehan, M., and Goodstein, J. (1993). Reasons for Staying Alive When You Are Thinking of Killing Yourself. *Journal of Consulting and Clinical Psychology, 51,* 276–286.

Sexual Activity Concerns

Myss, C. (1996). *Anatomy of the Spirit.* New York: Three Rivers Press.

Nevid, J. S., and Gotfried, F. (1995). *Choices: Sex in the Age of STDs.* Boston, MA: Allyn & Bacon.

Planned Parenthood: www.plannedparenthood.org.

Smith, S., and Smith, C. (1992). *College Student's Health Guide.* Los Altos, CA: Westchester Publishing Company.

Sternberg, R. (1988). *The Triangle of Love.* New York: Basic Books.

Sexual Identity Issues

Eichberg, R. (1991). *Coming Out: An Act of Love.* New York: Penguin.

Katz, J. (1996). *The Invention of Heterosexuality.* New York: Plume.

Marcus, E. (1993). *Is It a Choice? Answers to 300 of the Most Frequently Asked Questions About Gays and Lesbians*. San Francisco: HarperSanFrancisco.

Signorile, M. (1996). *Outing Yourself: How to Come Out as Lesbian or Gay to Your Family, Friends, and Coworkers*. New York: Fireside Books.

Suicidal Ideation

Hutschnecker, A. (1951). *The Will to Live*. New York: Cornerstone Library.

Linehan, M., and Goodstein, J. (1993). Reasons for Staying Alive When You Are Thinking of Killing Yourself. *Journal of Consulting and Clinical Psychology, 51,* 276–286.

Time Management

Burka, J. B., and Yuen, L. M. (1983). *Procrastination*. Cambridge, MA: Perseus Books.

Davidson, J. (2002). *The Complete Idiot's Guide to Managing Your Time*. Indianapolis, IN: Alpha Books.

Hettich, P. (1998). *Learning Skills for College and Career.* Pacific Grove, CA: Brooks/Cole Publishing Company.

Morgenstern, J. (1998). *Organizing from the Inside Out*. New York: Henry Holt and Company.

Morgenstern, J. (2000). *Time Management from the Inside Out*. New York: Henry Holt and Company.

Appendix C

INDEX OF *DSM-IV-TR* CODES ASSOCIATED WITH PRESENTING PROBLEMS

Academic Problem   **V62.3**
Academic Major Selection
Academic Underachievement
Graduation Anxiety
Learning/Physical Disabilities
Loneliness

Acculturation Problem   **V62.4**
Diversity Acceptance

Acute Stress Disorder   **308.3**
Abusive Relationships
Diversity Acceptance
Financial Stress
Graduation Anxiety
Loneliness
Pregnancy
Rape/Sexual Assault Victim
Sexual Activity Concerns

Adjustment Disorder   **309.xx**
Abusive Relationships
Childhood Abuse
Financial Stress
Loneliness

Adjustment Disorder with Anxiety   **309.24**
Abusive Relationships
Academic Major Selection
Academic Underachievement
Career Choice Confusion

Family Relationship Conflicts
Graduation Anxiety
Homesickness/Emancipation
  Issues
Intimacy/Commitment Issues
Pregnancy
Rape/Sexual Assault Victim
Roommate Conflicts
Sexual Identity Issues

Adjustment Disorder with Depressed Mood   **309.0**
Academic Major Selection
Career Choice Confusion
Depression
Graduation Anxiety
Grief/Loss
Homesickness/Emancipation
  Issues
Pregnancy
Rape/Sexual Assault Victim
Roommate Conflicts
Self-Esteem Deficit
Sexual Identity Issues

Adjustment Disorder with Disturbance of Conduct   **309.3**
Antisocial Behavior
Graduation Anxiety
Grief/Loss
Homesickness/Emancipation
  Issues
Roommate Conflicts

Childhood Abuse
Financial Stress
Graduation Anxiety
Homesickness/Emancipation
   Issues
Intimacy/Commitment Issues
Loneliness
Roommate Conflicts
Sexual Identity Issues

Hallucinogen Abuse   305.30
   Chemical Dependence/Abuse

Hallucinogen Dependence   304.50
   Chemical Dependence/Abuse

**Histrionic Personality
Disorder**   301.50
   Childhood Abuse
   Learning/Physical Disabilities
   Sexual Activity Concerns

Identity Problem   313.82
   Family Relationship Conflicts
   Graduation Anxiety
   Intimacy/Commitment Issues
   Sexual Activity Concerns
   Sexual Identity Issues

Impulse-Control Disorder   312.30
   Diversity Acceptance
   Self-Mutilation/Borderline
      Personality

Inhalant Abuse   305.90
   Chemical Dependence/Abuse

Inhalant Dependence   304.60
   Chemical Dependence/Abuse

**Intermittent Explosive
Disorder**   312.34
   Antisocial Behavior
   Childhood Abuse
   Learning/Physical Disabilities

Major Depressive Disorder   296.xx
   Self-Esteem Deficit

**Major Depressive Disorder,
Recurrent**   296.3x
   Depression
   Grief/Loss
   Self-Mutilation/Borderline
      Personality
   Sexual Identity Issues
   Suicidal Ideation

**Major Depressive Disorder,
Single Episode**   296.2x
   Abusive Relationships
   Childhood Abuse
   Depression
   Family Relationship Conflicts
   Grief/Loss
   Loneliness
   Self-Mutilation/Borderline
      Personality
   Sexual Identity Issues
   Suicidal Ideation

**Major Depressive Disorder,
Single Episode, Severe with
Psychotic Features**   296.24
   Psychotic Break

Malingering   V65.2
   Academic Major Selection

Mathematics Disorder   315.1
   Learning/Physical Disabilities

**Narcissistic Personality
Disorder**   301.81
   Antisocial Behavior
   Sexual Identity Issues

No Diagnosis or Condition   V71.09
   Abusive Relationships
   Academic Major Selection
   Academic Underachievement
   Antisocial Behavior
   Career Choice Confusion
   Chemical Dependence/Abuse
   Childhood Abuse
   Depression
   Diversity Acceptance
   Eating Disorders
   Family Relationship Conflicts
   Financial Stress